sponsored by

# the good
# Campaigns
## guide
### Campaigning for Impact

by Tess Kingham and Jim Coe

*voice of the voluntary sector*

The National Council for Voluntary Organisations (NCVO) is the umbrella body for the voluntary sector in England, with sister councils in Wales, Scotland and Northern Ireland. NCVO has a growing membership of over 3,600 voluntary organisations, ranging from large national bodies to community groups, volunteer bureaux and development agencies working at a local level. We work to support the voluntary sector and to create an environment in which voluntary organisations of all kinds can flourish by providing a wide range of information, advice and support services and by representing the views of the sector to government and policy makers.

**Our vision**
NCVO's vision is of a fair and open society, which encourages and is supported by voluntary action.

**Our mission**
NCVO aims:
• to give a shared voice to voluntary organisations
• to cultivate an environment that fosters their development
• to help voluntary organisations to achieve the highest standards of practice and effectiveness
• to provide leadership to the voluntary sector in tackling new issues and unmet needs

Published by NCVO Publications
(incorporating Bedford Square Press), imprint of the
National Council for Voluntary Organisations
Regent's Wharf, 8 All Saints Street, London N1 9RL

First published 2005

Typeset by JVT Design
Printed and bound by Latimer Trend and Co. Ltd.

British Library Cataloguing in Publication Data
A catalogue record for this book is available from the British Library

ISBN: 0 7199 1651 8

Every effort has been made to trace or contact the copyright holders of original text or illustrations used. The publishers will be pleased to correct any errors or omissions brought to their attention in future editions of this book.

"T'aint What You Do (It's The Way That Cha Do It)" – Words & Music by Sy Oliver & James Young. © Copyright 1939 MCA Music (a division of MCA Incorporated), USA. Universal/MCA Music Limited. Used by permission of Music Sales Limited. All Rights Reserved. International Copyright Secured.

"Waiting For The Great Leap Forwards" – Composed by Billy Bragg. Published by BMG Music Publishing Ltd. Used by permission. All rights reserved. © Billy Bragg.

"The Gambler" – written by Don Schlitz. Published by Sony/ATV Cross Keys Publishing. Used with permission. All rights reserved.

# Acknowledgements

Thanks to Mark Luetchford for supplying the Billy Bragg quote, plus many other things.

Thanks also to:

Jonathan Ellis at The Empty Homes Agency
Louise Hanson at Which?
Lisa Stacey at Barnardo's
Natasha Vromen at Drugscope
Richard English at Oxfam GB
John Grounds & Phillip Noyes at the NSPCC
Mike Hobday at the League Against Cruel Sports
Kate Green at the Child Poverty Action Group
Tim Linehan at The Children's Society
Jonathan Lomax at The Salvation Army
David Martin at Citizens Advice
Rowan Astbury at the Charities Evaluation Service
Nolan Quigley at NCVO
Brian Lamb at RNID

Thanks finally to Chris Stalker at NCVO for expert support and guidance.

# Contents

# Sponsor's Foreword

Abbey has been actively involved with the voluntary and community sector for many years and we are delighted to sponsor NCVO's *Good Campaigns Guide: Campaigning for Impact*. The sector is an integral part of the infrastructure of all active communities and acts as a catalyst for successful local regeneration, effective international aid and everything in between.

The publication of this practical guide coincides with major changes in charity legislation, the Year of the Volunteer and the impact on both business and the voluntary and community sector of the Government's Corporate Challenge. These, together with many other exciting changes and new opportunities, will have a significant and positive impact on the lives of the thousands of individuals and communities supported by voluntary action.

The guide explains how to influence different audiences and offers essential guidance on gaining the maximum impact. It goes on to examine the key issues in campaigning and offers insights into management, leadership and campaigning culture.

Armed with this guide all agencies working within the third sector can ensure that they are adopting the most effective tactics and campaigning mix to meet and overcome the challenges they face.

*Alan Eagle*

Alan Eagle
Manager
Charitable Trust
Abbey

**abbey**

For more information on Abbey's Charitable Trust please call
0870 608 0104

# Introduction

By Stuart Etherington
Chief Executive
NCVO

The voice of the voluntary and community sector is increasingly important to national life and campaigning represents a significant and growing part of the sector.

Campaigning fulfils all kinds of important functions in a flourishing democracy, from holding politicians to account to empowering the politically, economically and socially marginalised. Effective campaigning can make a key contribution to social and economic inclusion, building social capital, generating voluntary action and promoting sustainable community development.

It is vital that those within the sector who seek to represent the opinions of, and affect the lives of, citizens – through engagement with powerful UK and international political and economic institutions – do so efficiently, effectively and in an accountable way.

Campaigning continues to be a developing discipline. NCVO's experience is that there are pockets of excellence within the campaigning sub-sector and significant good work being carried out. However, opportunities to share learning, especially across sub-sectors, are very limited and we see a number of common issues facing voluntary and community sector campaigning organisations. The publication of this book is extremely well timed as it identifies and builds on existing good practice and seeks to share it with those committed to planning and delivering high-impact campaigns within the voluntary and community sector.

I sincerely hope you find it interesting, relevant and useful.

## Who is this guide for?

Anyone involved in improving campaigning effectiveness, including:

- the trustees who govern campaigning organisations;
- the management team, who must work with trustees to formulate policy, represent their members and influence decision makers;
- the staff and volunteers who require clear plans and strategies in order to fulfil their day-to-day roles; and
- the team within the organisation who work on campaigns.

Whatever your status or setting we hope that you find this book useful and thought provoking.

## Making the most of this book

### Case studies
Case studies are used throughout this book and are shaded in grey. They illustrate ideas and approaches to dealing with real-life situations.

### Key learning points
These are identified at the end of each chapter and are designed to encourage you to move straight from theory into practice.

### Other NCVO Good Guides
This book is the part of series of Good Guides published by NCVO. The other guides include: *The Good Management Guide*; *The Good Financial Management Guide*; *The Good Employment Guide*; *The Good Membership Guide*; *The Good Trustee Guide*; and *The Good Investment Guide*. Some of the themes in this guide overlap with those in other good guides – where this happens we will signpost you to the relevant publication. Find out more at www.ncvo-vol.org.uk/publications.

### NCVO Forums
NCVO runs a range of networking groups, covering specific areas of work. Particularly relevant to readers of this Guide are the PWG (Parliamentary Workers Group), PR Forum (Public Relations and Press Officers) and the EuroGroup (EU Officers). Find out more at www.ncvo-vol.org.uk/networks or call NCVO's HelpDesk on 0800 2 798 798.

### Your feedback please!
Finally, we would appreciate your feedback to help ensure that future editions of *The Good Campaigns Guide* are as relevant as possible. Please fill in the feedback form at the back of this book or email publications@ncvo-vol.org.uk.

# Preface

Campaigning is about change.

All campaigns, protests and movements depend on people organising themselves to effect change in their communities – to have an impact.

With comparatively tiny resources, during its long history the voluntary and community sector (VCS) in the UK has achieved massive impact through its campaigning. And the protests and causes of the past are echoed in today's campaigns. The abolition of child labour in 19th century Britain finds an echo in the Fair Trade movement of today. The fight for women's right to vote is reflected in today's work for gender equality. The ideals behind the promotion of allotments in the 19th century can be found in the organic food movement of the 21st century. There are parallels in the protests of the conscientious objectors of the First World War with the mass protests about the recent war in Iraq. Whether waged by the co-operative pioneers of over a hundred years ago or anti-globalisation protestors today, the fight of those who care about justice and equality continues. From the campaign for horse-trough provision in Victorian cities to campaigns against worldwide habitat destruction; from clean air campaigns to international action against climate change – the world changes but there will always be more campaigns to wage.

## Definitions

When we talk about campaigns in this book, we mean organised actions around a specific issue seeking to bring about changes in the policy and behaviours of institutions and/or specific public groups.

When we talk about campaigning, we mean the mobilising of forces by organisations to influence others in order to effect an identified and desired social, economic, environmental or political change.

We use both terms in a broad sense, i.e. campaigns and campaigning can incorporate one or more of the following elements:

- targeted lobbying and influencing strategies directed towards decision makers;
- organising people to take action and demonstrate concern;
- raising the public profile of issues and messages.

So campaigning is about having impact; it is about changing people's lives. But change is complicated and to achieve it campaigners in the VCS often seek to combat and counter powerful vested interests.

Successful campaigners fight passionately for what they believe is a just cause, but not just that. Outside the VCS, the word campaign has two resonances – military and advertising – and campaigners should learn from both. Military and advertising campaigns are carefully planned and executed. They take care to match resources, actions and objectives. They manage to combine strategic planning with flexibility of response.

This book articulates a way of thinking about campaigning in the VCS that seeks to transfer this basic thinking. It is based on the premise that campaigns are most successful when they combine strategic astuteness and tactical opportunism. The best campaigners make this look deceptively simple but they have not always been good at sharing their learning.

This book is not so much about the detailed mechanics of a campaign: there are plenty of other sources of information about the best ways to organise a public meeting, write a press release or undertake direct action. Instead this book is about developing strategic thinking around campaigns and campaigning.

Campaigning has not yet developed fully as a professional discipline (in the same way as charity fundraising for instance) but it is moving in that direction and this book is a small contribution to that task.

Remember that the resources of those who oppose your arguments, or who find it convenient merely to ignore you, are often vast. Operating in often contested and controversial arenas, campaigners will need to be increasingly sophisticated at identifying goals, developing innovative influencing techniques, seizing opportunities and rebutting attacks. It is incumbent on the VCS to do all that it can to ensure it gets better at campaigning to have real impact. To do this, campaigners may have to take a step back and rethink their approach.

Campaigners have traditionally brought enthusiasm and verve to the VCS and have already achieved some major social, economic and political change. It is hoped that this book will help to harness this dynamism to achieve even greater impact.

The Good Campaigns Guide is organised into five parts.

Parts one and two concentrate on campaigns. Parts four and five concentrate on campaigning. Part three provides a useful summary and acts as a link between these two themes. It is intended to bridge the two halves of the book together.

Part one – sets out the premise that campaigning must focus on achieving impact.
Part two – explains the campaign cycle and provides a series of tools to develop and run campaigns to achieve impact
Part three – provides a useful and short summary which links parts one and two to parts four and five
Part four – examines how your organisation could improve its approach to campaigning.
Part five – explores the understanding of how change happens and how this could further influence the development of individual campaigns and campaigning organisations.

# Part one: Campaigning for impact

_____

**… in which we explain the premise that campaigning must focus on achieving impact.**

# I Campaigning and impact

> "That Alchemy is a pretty kind of game,
> somewhat like tricks o' the cards, to cheat a man
> With charming."
> **Ben Jonson, The Alchemist**

## 1.1 Planning for impact

Campaigners are modern alchemists. They seek to change a few basic raw materials into something magical. Yet the best campaigners must be better at achieving results than the men and women who strove to turn base material into the philosophers' stone.

Campaigning, unlike alchemy, is a relatively new phenomenon. In the long-term, alchemists like Isaac Newton laid the basis for modern science; we believe today's campaigners are in a similar position. They are laying the foundations of new ways of looking at how to effect change.

We aim to enable campaigners, as modern alchemists, to use their skill, judgement and energy to transform available resources into positive social change.

Good campaigners analyse, make plans, act and have an impact.

It is a simple process, which looks like this:

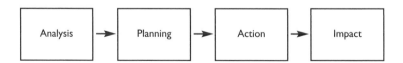

We define
impact as
"significant
or lasting
changes in
people's lives,
brought
about by a
given action,
or series of
actions".

---

**Impact**

We define impact as "significant or lasting changes in people's lives, brought about by a given action, or series of actions".[1] This definition is important because it identifies the ultimate goal of campaigning in relation to changes in people's lives. Changes in institutional policies and practice, for example, should be seen as means to that end, not ends in themselves. Effective campaigning is about impact not action, results not effort, outcomes not outputs.

---

As experienced campaigners, we have over the last 15 years or so developed some ideas and tools to help navigate this process in order to maximise impact. They are designed to be equally applicable to the beginner with very limited resources and the seasoned campaigner with a large organisation behind her or him.

Effective campaigning involves using the minimum amount of effort to achieve the maximum impact. In thinking about the best way to achieve this, here are some of the factors that may need to be addressed:

- external factors play a significant role in the campaigning environment – you need to try to predict how things are likely to evolve (e.g. what kind of response your campaign might get) through sound preparation.
- resources can be organised in many different ways, and those you are seeking to change can be influenced in many different ways; analysis will help think through some of the best routes to take – to make an informed judgement.
- identifying how best to reach your end goal and therefore the changes you are seeking to achieve along the route need to be defined (e.g. to be influential, is one meeting with officials necessary or are a thousand people protesting outside the ministry needed?)

We advocate dealing with these factors by giving particular attention to the early stages of campaign planning. The danger is that if insufficient thought is given to planning, or an inappropriate approach is adopted, your campaigning effort will not have the desired impact.

We have seen too much creative energy wasted. And the result of this is frustrating for campaigners but, more importantly, what we should never forget is why we campaign in the first place.

Whether or not we express it in these terms, we are trying to make the world, or at least a small part of it, a better place. This is a big prize. It would be irresponsible not to go about it in the most effective manner possible.

## 1.2 The impact chain

The mechanics of campaigning can be made simple if you understand the principle of the impact chain.

This is a model that breaks down the process of change into component parts.

A simple model of change looks like this:

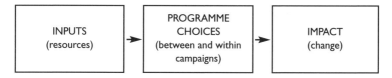

The impact chain breaks down the process of change into component parts and, in doing so, makes a distinction between different levels of change:

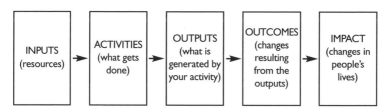

Understanding the impact chain is a good first step in effective campaigning.

To create an impact at the end of the chain you need to make the right choice at the beginning of the chain. In effect all campaigning is about making choices. Make the right choice and it will achieve impact: make the wrong choice and (unless you extract learning from your mistake) you are wasting your time, someone else's money and everyone's opportunity.

Assumptions about how change happens are inherent in all the choices you have to make. You need to be informed about what are the right choices to make. You need to make the assessment.

You then need to marshal your resources – to make plans to take that choice. Then you need to act to make the choice and finally you need to ensure you have had an impact.

We make choices like this all the time – largely intuitively. Feel hungry, check you have enough money in your pocket, go to a shop, buy the right amount of food, eat it, feel full. If you forget your money or you don't have any you won't be able to buy the food when you get to the checkout.

Also, if you choose to do one thing, you can't do another – if you go to a shop to buy food you can't go to a restaurant at exactly the same time. You need to assess the choice you have made.

If you spend time organising a press conference to launch a new report it's because you believe this to be a better use of your time than sending out a mailing to supporters asking them to write to their Member of Parliament asking her or him to read the report.

One benefit of using the impact chain as the starting point for thinking about campaigning for impact is that it makes explicit – and draws out – the assumptions underlying these kinds of choices.

The impact chain provides a tool for investigating whether assumptions about how change happens make sense. It helps to ensure that choices are well thought out and thus achieve greater impact than other possible choices.

**The impact chain provides a tool for investigating whether assumptions about how change happens make sense.**

## 1.3 Outputs, outcomes and impact

The important lesson from the impact chain is the distinction between outputs and outcomes. To return to the example of feeling hungry, if you choose to buy a meal that does not satisfy your hunger that means although you have achieved the output you have not affected an outcome and hence had no impact.

Often campaigners in the voluntary and community sector instinctively concentrate on outputs, that is the amount of activity generated. It is easy to measure how many meetings are organised, how many press interviews are held, or how many postcards are delivered. The more pertinent questions to ask are, 'What are the outcomes of this activity? What are the results of what we are doing? Are they achieving an impact?'

## Understanding the impact chain

| stage | short explanation | assumptions in the process | degree of control |
|---|---|---|---|
| **INPUTS** [resources] | The resources you put in – time, money and expertise. | certain resources are needed for your campaign ... | *your planned work; within internal control* |
| **ACTIVITIES** [what gets done] | What you actually do with the available resources day-to-day. Campaigns will tend to involve a mix of lobbying, media and popular campaigning actions but the balance between these different activities will depend on the issue, the ultimate goal and the context in which the campaign takes place. | ... if you have access to these resources then you can use them to accomplish a range of activities ... | |
| **OUTPUTS** [what is generated by activity] | Your actions measured and monitored. For example, x number of meetings with ministers and officials, y thousands of signatures on a petition, z amount of media coverage. | ... if you accomplish these activities, you will deliver a certain set of results ... | |
| **OUTCOMES** [changes resulting from the outputs] | The milestones of change. Impact will be your final goal (see below) but the outcomes plot the steps along the way to this. In the short term, this might involve, for example, parts of the media taking up your issue, or a government spokesperson issuing a public statement about it (even if it is not supportive of your goals). In the longer term, you could see the government taking steps to change the way legislation is being enacted. | ... if you deliver these results, then you will help to achieve change in the ways that certain publics or institutions regard a particular issue and how they behave in relation to it ... | *your intended results; subject to increasing external influence* |
| **IMPACT** [changes in people's lives] | How have things changed as a result of your campaign? What are the significant or lasting changes in people's lives to which your actions have contributed? Do these changes truly benefit your client groups? How do they affect others? | ... if you achieve these changes, benefits will accrue to those whom you represent – on whose behalf you are campaigning ... | |

**Distinction between outputs, outcomes and impact**

| Stage in the change process | What is being measured? |
|---|---|
| Outputs | Effort – i.e. what is generated as a result of your activities |
| Outcomes | Effects – i.e. what changes result in the short- and long-term resulting from these outputs |
| Impact | Change – i.e. the lasting or significant changes in people's lives that result from these outcomes |

**Focusing your attention on the effects of your efforts – the outcomes – should help you think about how effective you are being**

Getting stuck at thinking about outputs means concentrating on effort. Effort is important but it must be focused to be effective. Focusing your attention on the effects of your efforts – the outcomes – should help you think about how effective you are being, and, ultimately, whether your campaigning is making an impact.

The purpose of adopting this kind of model as a way of looking at campaigning is to ensure that you do not focus too much on outputs. People can march through the streets of London but, if those organising the demonstration have merely been thinking about the output (numbers of people), there may not be an outcome in terms of effect and therefore no subsequent impact in terms of change.

Too many people forget this in their rush to get things done.

To campaign successfully without having thought about the impact of what you are planning is not impossible but it is more difficult than people often realise. It is definitely more difficult to sustain and to succeed.

**Headless Chicken Syndrome**

Chickens need heads. If you cut them off, proverbially they run around aimlessly. In reality they probably fall over quite quickly.

Too many campaigners waste a lot of their time running around frantically doing too many things with little or no thought about their impact. They sometimes get lucky and have an impact. But too often they get frustrated and go off and do something else or the campaign loses its dynamism.

Although Mike the Headless Chicken apparently survived without a head and toured America in a modern freak show for over a year in 1945, most campaigners probably want their career to last for longer than that.

The campaign cycle described in this book provides one framework for thinking through some of the key areas likely to affect the course of a particular campaign.

It seeks to suggest that campaigning should be focused on impact.

The best way to have impact is to plan for impact.

## Learning point

You may wish to consider the following:

- ✓ Campaign outputs need to effect outcomes to have an impact.
- ✓ Do you understand the principle of the impact chain?
- ✓ Do you understand the difference between outputs, outcomes and impact?

1 from Roche, C (1999) *Impact Assessment for Development Agencies: Learning to Value Change*. Oxfam

# Part two:
# The campaign cycle

**... in which the campaign cycle is explained and a series of tools are provided to help develop and run campaigns to achieve impact.**

# 2  Introducing the campaign cycle

He will win who knows when to fight, and when not to fight
He will win who knows how to handle both superior and
inferior forces
He will win whose army is animated by the same spirit
throughout its ranks
He will win who, prepared himself, waits to take the enemy
unprepared
He will win who has military capacity and is not interfered with
by the sovereign
Victory lies in the knowledge of these five points.
Hence the saying: If you know the enemy and know yourself, you
need not fear
the result of a hundred battles.
**Sun Tzu, The Art of War**

## 2.1 The argument for planning

Campaigning is an active and dynamic discipline. As a result, many campaigners like to follow their gut instinct, seize opportunities as they arise and adapt tactics as they go. They believe that campaigners should act fast and furiously. Our experience is that many of the most successful campaigns (including some highlighted as case studies in this book) are driven by people who have an intuitive grasp of the best ways to effect change in any particular situation. No one should deny the creative side of campaigning.

Unfortunately, in our experience, many of the most unsuccessful campaigns are based on a so-called 'intuitive approach' that is not focused, and not built on a thorough understanding of policy making and political processes.

The danger is that, if you campaign in this way you will rush around doing lots of things but without getting anywhere, like the proverbial headless chicken.

As evaluators, the authors often see the greatest weaknesses in the ways that campaigns are designed and developed occurring in their early stages. Early lapses in thinking through the options can have a knock-on detrimental effect on how the campaign develops, leading, for example, to lack of clarity about the aim of the campaign and the best way to achieve this aim. The result can be that organisations are not using resources most effectively – and remember that even the biggest organisation almost certainly has only relatively few resources compared to the size of the task they are taking on.

In art foundation courses, students typically learn pencil drawing. This is not because the skills of drawing with pencils will necessarily be utilised after graduation, but because drawing helps develop a new way of seeing the world. In the same way, the campaign cycle is a way of promoting a **way of thinking** about the discipline of campaigning.

**The campaign cycle is a way of promoting a way of thinking about the discipline of campaigning.**

> Remember the campaign cycle is intended as only one possible guide through the complexities of campaign planning. We think it is more important to apply the general principles than simply to follow the model that we are describing, or to use the specific tools that we depict.

**As a planning tool to think through the routes to impact, the campaign cycle can be adopted.**

The idea of the impact chain has already been introduced. This is a way of thinking about how change happens, and the levels of change that a campaign can achieve. It is not a planning tool but is designed to help you understand that the overall principle of campaigning is based on making choices to achieve impact. As a planning tool to think through the routes to impact, the campaign cycle can be adopted.

**The campaign cycle**

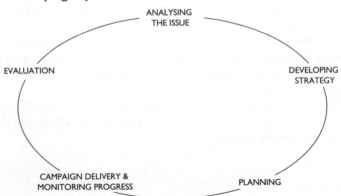

ANALYSING THE ISSUE

EVALUATION

DEVELOPING STRATEGY

CAMPAIGN DELIVERY & MONITORING PROGRESS

PLANNING

This is an unsophisticated but effective model – the equivalent of learning to ride a bicycle. The rest of Part Two of this book takes you on a functional cycle ride around this circle, from analysis to evaluation.

An understanding of this simple campaign cycle will:

- help emphasise the concept of campaigning as an integrated process – from start (understanding the issue) to finish (evaluation) and then back to the start again!
- provide you with a touchstone – so you can identify where you are in the campaigning process at any given time and anticipate what you should do next.
- offer a useful framework for planning your campaigns, helping you to retain focus, direct limited resources where impact is likely to be greatest and monitor the campaign at given stages to alter its course if necessary.

## 2.3 The stages in design, development and planning

This campaign cycle involves five stages:

1. Analysing the issue and the context
   - understanding the issue
   - examining the external factors that affect your campaign
   - examining the internal factors that affect your campaign

2. Developing the campaign strategy
   - selecting the solution
   - setting the campaign aim
   - framing the campaign
   - identifying routes of influence
   - identifying steps to influence policy makers

3. Setting objectives
   - setting clear, measurable objectives
   - establishing a monitoring and evaluation framework
   - developing workplans
   - testing the plan
   - contingency planning

4. Delivering and monitoring the campaign
   - understanding your audiences
   - identifying the campaign mix
   - devising tactics
   - communicating with your audiences
   - managing the campaign

5. Evaluating the campaign
   * timetabling evaluations

## Learning point

You may wish to consider the following:

✓ Managing a campaign based on the idea of a campaign cycle can help direct limited resources towards greatest impact.

# 3 Analysing the issue and the context

"Behavior at the board can easily be separated into making moves and shifting checkers ... Decisions as to which move to make are problematic and significant; pushing the checker once the decision is made is neither."
**Erving Goffman, Framing Analysis**

## 3.1 Understanding the issue

Voluntary and community organisations [VCOs] usually have a clear idea of the issues that affect them, their work and what they want to do about them.

VCOs usually know what they want to change and how to do it. Or do they?

One criticism frequently levelled at VCOs is that they are very good at publicising the terrible state of the world but often unclear and unspecific about what they want done to put it right.

Members of Parliament and other policy makers have told us that VCOs usually approach them and ask them simply to 'take up an issue'. This is not very useful. Policy makers need specifics – they need to know exactly what causes the problem, clear evidence to back up the case and proposed solutions. These solutions should preferably be tried and tested so it is easier to convince others to adopt them.

So why is there a tendency for VCOs, who are so expert at providing a service to their client base (many even very good at carrying out complex policy analysis), to be so vague and unstrategic when approaching policy makers with solutions?

It seems that quite often it is the very complexity of the issues that fazes people. We think we know the problem but when we try to unravel it to find clear solutions, it's like unravelling a tangled spring – it is forever winding back on itself and getting ever more tangled.

So there is a need for a way to deconstruct complex problems and issues and to identify specific solutions that are achievable within the political contexts campaigns operate in.

**Policy makers need specifics – they need to know exactly what causes the problem, clear evidence to back up the case and proposed solutions.**

For your campaign to have focus you need to answer the following key questions:
1. What is the nature of the problems you wish to solve?
2. What are their causes and consequences?
3. What is the range of possible solutions available to you?

## A problem and solution tree

A useful tool for thinking through these questions and identifying a range of solutions is a problem and solution tree, compiled as follows:

### Problem tree

Clearly and simply state the problem you wish to resolve in the box in the centre of the tree. Involve all relevant stakeholders in discussing the problem, focusing on the questions below:

What are the causes of the problem? There may be several inter-related causes or just one.

What are the consequences 'on the ground' of this problem? How does it affect those you work with?

Write the causes of the problem in the boxes at the bottom of the problem tree and the consequences (the effects) in the boxes above the tree.

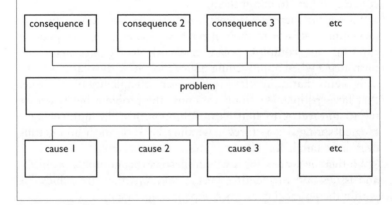

**Turning your problem tree into a solution tree**

Discuss the ideal situation you would like to reach. Now write this 'vision' on a piece of paper and stick it over the 'problem' in the centre of the tree.

For each of the causes of the problem (as written in the boxes below the tree) discuss and identify a potential solution. The following questions may help:
- What policy or practice would need to change for the solution to be reached?
- What specifically needs to happen?
- Who can bring about the change? For example government, parliament, civil servants, donors.

Write the solutions on paper and stick them over the causes.

Now discuss how the solutions would improve the situation. What would the positive outcomes be? Write these outcomes on paper and stick them over the consequences in the boxes above the tree.

You have now transformed your problem into a range of potential solutions. One or some of these solutions may be the ones you campaign for.

## 3.2 Analysing the context

VCOs often lay claim to the moral high ground on issues they want to address – but it is incumbent on them to remember that they do not operate in a vacuum.

Outside your organisations, the world of the policy makers works to its own timetable, its own priorities and at a pace you cannot dictate. If you are to get your issue on the agenda, it is important to spend time analysing what is happening externally.

A little introspection to make sure you have the capacity and the legitimacy to campaign effectively on your identified solutions may also be helpful. This need not be a gargantuan task but simply asking yourselves some pertinent questions and pinpointing any areas of weakness you need to address to get on the right track. The following sections and checklists might help to analyse the context in which you are campaigning.

> The world of the policy makers works to its own timetable, its own priorities and at a pace you cannot dictate.

## 3.3 External analysis – the world outside

Unless you understand the world you are operating in and the political dynamics of the situation you wish to influence, you cannot target your campaign effectively and efficiently.

> ### Reviewing the context
>
> Periods of reflection can be valuable, not just at the beginning of a campaign, but at key moments within its development.
>
> The Child Poverty Action Group's [CPAG] analysis, for example, is that the Labour government in the UK has been broadly sympathetic to the child poverty agenda. Their key concern in late 2004 was how investment in tackling child poverty could be sustained, given shifting economic and political contexts and with the likelihood of a general election in the first six months of 2005. External changes may entail a different campaigning approach. In thinking about the next phase of the campaign, therefore, questions to consider include:
>
> - how is the debate going? who is saying what?
> - how are the political parties' shifting positioning affecting the way they address child poverty issues?
> - what are likely to be the priorities of the next Parliament?
> - who will be the key players?
> - who will attack CPAG's positions and how can such attacks be rebutted?
> - what kinds of approaches will work politically in the next Parliament?
>
> CPAG is seeking to shape the political parties' pre-election considerations (through influencing their manifestos for example), but is otherwise deliberately biding its time, testing the political water for the next phase of the campaign.

For your campaign to have focus, you need to be able answer the following key questions:
- What are the political dynamics of the situation?
- What other external circumstances may affect the campaign goal?
- Is the external climate favourable or hostile to your proposed solutions?

## A PEST analysis

An easily manageable way of sifting through this mass of information is to construct a PEST analysis, which involves looking at the political, economic, social and technical factors likely to influence your campaigning. The kinds of questions you should ask include the following:

**Do you understand the political climate within which you operate?**
- What are the national/regional/local policy-making structures that affect your issue and how will decision making work in this instance?
- Which political players are likely to be friends, foes or floaters?
- Is your contact base with decision makers strong?
- Are there any political developments pending that could influence the outcome of your campaign or polarise political opinion for or against you?

**Will economic conditions affect your campaign?**
- Will the economic climate influence government spending to benefit/threaten your desired outcomes?
- If you are working with the corporate sector, are economic issues/forecasts likely to affect their actions?

**What social factors could influence your work?**
- Is public opinion generally with you or against you on this issue?
- How do the media cover this issue – positive/negative/undecided?
- Are other civil society organisations supportive of your aims?
- Which other influentials stand with you or against you (do you have celebrity or 'hero' figures with you)?
- Does your desired outcome have other social knock-on effects?

**What are the technical/scientific influences on your campaign?**
- Is there scientific evidence stacked against your argument? If so, can you counter it?
- Changing communications technology may provide different routes to influence targets. Are there recent developments in communications technology that have a bearing on how you conduct your campaign?

## 3.4 Internal analysis – is this campaign right for you?

**For a campaign to be charitable, it will need to be demonstrably linked to the achievement of charitable objectives.**

Time dedicated to assessing whether you and your organisation have the capacity to undertake your chosen campaign, and whether the issue is suitable for your organisation, is time well spent.

If you have charitable status, this must be taken into account. Your trustees are tasked with ensuring that the organisation does not deviate from its charitable objects. For a campaign to be charitable, it will need to be demonstrably linked to the achievement of charitable objectives.

Even if your organisation is not subject to charity law, it will probably have an organisational strategy within which your campaigning must fit. Campaigning activity is also subject to the law of the land, although some organisations are not afraid to make illegal activity part of their campaigns. All of this needs to be taken into account when carrying out an internal analysis.

Answering the following key questions may help:
- Does your organisation have legitimacy for this campaign?
- Are you prepared for the campaign?
- Can you deliver adequate resources?

---

Why not ask yourselves the following?

**Legitimacy?**
- For whom do you speak and have they been involved in the process?
- To whom are you accountable and does this bear scrutiny?
- Do you speak with authority? Do you have hands-on experience of the issue or a track record in this area?
- What are your fault-lines? Your opponents will find them and exploit your weaknesses so anticipate and prepare a defence.

**Capacity?**
- Are management and decision-making systems efficient and effective?
- Is there stakeholder buy-in within and outside the organisation?
- Have you considered the implications of the campaign for your reputation, positioning and operations (for example funder reaction)?
- Are there risk factors for your wider work?

---

**Resources?**
- What are the staffing and budget implications? If the campaign 'takes-off', for how long can you sustain activity?
- Do you need to raise additional funds for the campaign?

## A SWOT summary: pulling the thinking together

One helpful way of categorising the information derived from your internal and external analyses is in the form of a SWOT summary.

SWOT stands for strengths, weaknesses, opportunities and threats to your organisation. SWOTs are usually laid out on a grid.

### New hospital for Gloucester

During 1997, the newly-elected MP for Gloucester (co-author of this book) led a campaign to persuade the new Government to rebuild the city's hospital. Knowing that competition was fierce, the campaign team carried out a thorough PEST analysis (see page 29), compiled a SWOT from this and used it to formulate the campaign strategy. A summary version is included below:

Strengths
- Strong legitimacy – wide public support (patients, clinical staff, VCOs)
- Excellent cross-media buy-in (local daily newspaper, radio)
- Hospital developed strong clinical case with sound evidence
- Hospital site spacious and adaptable
- Efficient campaign liaison team (from hospital, daily newspaper, MP office)
- Gloucester was 1997 election 'barometer' seat
- Labour-controlled city council supportive
- Good relations with health minister

Weaknesses
- Local delays in drawing up bid
- Hospital size – borderline for Private Finance Initiative [PFI] project
- Cheltenham/Gloucester hospitals merger discussions ongoing
- Government decision making opaque
- Perceived lukewarm support from County Council
- Perceived lukewarm support from Regional Health Authority
- No dedicated budget

Opportunities
- Prime Minister promised new hospital during pre-election visit (find witnesses!)
- Cross-media campaign – mass public petitioning for PM to keep promise
- MP's first 100 days – media interest in Gloucester – exploit it
- Comparisons with other cities – fair shares for Gloucester
- Lobby Health Minister direct via MP
- Government second wave hospital programme launched
- Good range of support – use strategically

Threats
- County competition – some supposed political 'allies' see Gloucester as threat
- Some trades union disquiet about PFI and impact on members
- City Council elections could overturn Labour majority
- Intense competition in Parliament from 'colleagues' also wanting hospitals

The SWOT highlighted several key points for the campaign liaison team:

1. The clinical case was strong but there was intense political competition.
2. The Prime Minister's pre-election promise could give Gloucester political advantage over competitors if used skilfully with the media
3. Allies cannot be assumed. It was a shock to discover that another Labour MP from the county was not, as

> supposed, totally supportive. Presumably concerned that her area would lose out if Gloucester gained, she was privately undermining the campaign with the relevant Minister.
> 4. Some key stakeholders – trades unions – had legitimate and serious concerns that needed to be considered when developing the campaign 'solution'.

By categorising the answers to the questions above as strengths, weaknesses, opportunities or threats for your campaign and placing them in a SWOT summary, you will identify the problematic areas at an early stage and be able to address them.

## Learning points

You may wish to consider the following:

✓ Effective campaigns are based on a good understanding of the context in which they function
✓ Be specific – policy makers need to know what causes the problem. Have you got evidence to back up your case and proposed solutions?
✓ Have you identified the nature of the problems you wish to solve and what are their causes and consequences?
✓ What is the range of possible solutions available to you?
✓ Have you identified the political dynamics of the situation?
✓ What other external circumstances may affect your campaign goal?
✓ Is the external climate favourable or hostile to your proposed solutions?
✓ Would a PEST or a SWOT analysis be useful?

# 4 Developing strategy

"You got to know when to hold 'em, know when to fold 'em,
Know when to walk away and know when to run.
You never count your money when you're sittin' at the table,
There'll be time enough for countin' when the dealin's done."
**Kenny Rogers, *The Gambler***

## 4.1 Selecting the right solution

Choosing the right solution is vital because it influences the whole direction of your campaign. If your solution is unsuitable or unachievable, you risk pouring a lot of resources into a bottomless pit.

By now, you will have considered the problem, identified a range of possible solutions and developed an understanding of the internal and external contexts in which you are operating. You can now use this information to decide which solution is the best to campaign on.

For your campaign to have focus, you need to be able to answer the following key questions:
- if achieved, which solution offers the greatest potential impact for your client group; in other words, will it make a difference?
- given the SWOT summary, which solution appears most achievable; in other words, is it winnable?

There is likely to be a trade off between these two.

If you can find a solution where the benefit is likely to be substantial and your analysis suggests that it is easily winnable, you have identified the holy grail of campaigning and you should go for it with all the enthusiasm and resources you can muster. In most cases, though, it is likely that the solutions that deliver the greatest benefits will be the most difficult to achieve. You will need to make a judgement and get as close to the ideal as possible.

**It is likely that the solutions that deliver the greatest benefits will be the most difficult to achieve.**

## Selecting the issue

Two key factors underpinned the decision by Citizens Advice to select as a major campaigning focus the issue of tenants being denied a return of their deposits.

1. There had been clear evidence coming from the network of Citizens Advice Bureaux over the last decade or more that this was a major and consistent concern raised by those seeking support and advice. Many tenants in private rented accommodation were finding that landlords were withholding deposits at the end of the tenancy without good reason, and the opportunities for redress were inadequate.
2. Coupled with this, the government had taken some steps to address the issue, by funding and evaluating a three-year pilot scheme. A key political opportunity to make further policy progress presented itself with the announcement of a Housing Bill in the 2003 Queen's Speech.

Citizens Advice joined forces with Shelter to launch the Tenancy Deposits Campaign in response to these twin strands, one relating to the potential impact on beneficiaries that resolution would bring and the other relating to the assessment that there was good prospect of making progress on the issue at that particular time.

## What makes a campaign winnable?

There is no set formula to follow, but a combination of the following is likely to be helpful:
- the ability to assign responsibility for the current situation to a clear target
- obvious influencing opportunities
- the ability to tap into a sense of deeply and/or widely felt public outrage
- an issue that grabs the attention
- a sense of urgency and importance
- a short and clear causal story – it is easier to explain how landmines maim and kill innocent civilians than it

is to explain the concept that the International Monetary Fund's policies are responsible for causing food riots in a particular country for example

- a group of potential beneficiaries who have particular electoral influence.

In addition to these 'campaignability' factors, it is likely to help if you are prepared to be pragmatic about what campaign victory might look like, by

- offering solutions or remedies that are politically attractive to decision makers
- being willing to negotiate an outcome.

Along with this, our judgement is that when you identify a campaign you should include an organisational commitment to campaign on the issue until it is resolved.

**When you identify a campaign you should include an organisational commitment to campaign on the issue until it is resolved.**

## 4.2 Setting the campaign aim

Once you have pinpointed the solution you wish to achieve, a clear campaign aim will act as a beacon towards which everyone involved in the campaign should head.

It is surprising how few campaigns have this basic element. Our experience is that the campaigns that do have an aim usually succeed in focusing effort on achieving impact. Campaigns that either don't have an aim, or have a poorly defined one, are usually poorly focused.

The aim is the headline statement that encapsulates the ultimate purpose of the campaign. It should be communicated easily and succinctly to anyone who wants to know about it, from the media interviewer to the politician, or internally to your own staff.

Without a single aim, people (including staff internally) may be unclear as to why you are doing what you are doing.

In setting the aim, you need answer the following key questions:

- who needs to change for the desired solution to be achieved? (This individual or group is the target of your campaign.)
- what needs to be different?

If there is more than one ultimate target, you need two aims. Usually if you need two aims, you need two campaigns; three aims, three campaigns – and so on.

A campaign aim is best when it is:
- succinct – able to be summed up in one sentence
- compelling and inspiring – conveying the moral force of the issue
- easily communicated
- targeted – identifying who needs to change, and how they should change, for the campaign to be successful
- impact focused – articulating the need for a change that, when achieved, will directly lead to an improvement in people's lives.

---

### Campaigning and language[1] – the landmines campaign

One cited reason for the success of the international campaign to ban landmines was that those who were campaigning against landmines took the argument away from the technical experts – by describing landmines in terms of a humanitarian, not a military, issue. The decision was taken to call publicly for a ban on landmines because they killed and maimed farmers rather than the less engaging call for the regulation of use, sale, stockpiling and manufacture of anti-personnel mines.

It is true that the argument about banning landmines was effectively about disarmament. But by keeping the focus of the debate on the practical consequences of real human suffering and away from arguments relating to the theory of warfare and deterrence (the preferred realm of government experts) campaigners pushed the issue higher up and further along the political agenda.

---

It is important that you do not confuse your aim and your objectives. You may need to meet several objectives, each of which may act as stepping-stones to achieving the overall aim, but you will have only one campaign aim.

## Campaign aim

Full Stop provides for the NSPCC the overarching framework for its campaigning and programme work. Encompassed within Full Stop are a range of campaigns that each make a contribution to the NSPCC's mission – to end cruelty to children in the UK.

Under the Full Stop umbrella, the NSPCC runs public campaigns on issues including physical punishment, sexual abuse and child abuse deaths, for example, as well as more targeted lobbying and influencing in support of key provisions within the legislative programme.

Each of these specific campaigns has an aim. To take one example, the NSPCC's aim in its campaign on child abuse deaths is for the government to establish, and outline steps towards meeting targets to reduce the national incidence of child deaths through abuse.

## Is your campaign charitable?

If political activity still worries you because your organisation has charitable status, now is the time to make sure you have checked the campaign aim against the obligations that go with that status. See the Appendix (page 209) on charitable law to consider the impact charitable status has on your ability to campaign

Now it is important to build on the aim by:
1. framing the campaign; and
2. identifying routes of influence.

### 4.3 Framing the campaign

All issues are 'framed' in some way – that is they are packaged and presented. The issues you want to campaign on have usually been already framed by others.

The way your opponents or even those who are simply resistant to your message frame it, can have an influence on the policy makers you wish to influence. Your challenge then is to frame or reframe the issue so that people think about it in different ways and policy makers perceive the issue in a way that suits your interests.[2]

---

Framing the issue – how to do it:
- deliver it in clear and engaging language
- give your analysis of the problem and its cause, identifying those responsible for the problem, showing why a given state is neither natural nor accidental
- outline the evidence for the problem – including a human story
- dramatise the concern – show it to be important, urgent and compelling
- present clear and credible solutions, showing whom you hold responsible for solving the problem
- state the actions you ask others to take in support of the solution

---

You could use a grid like this:

| The Problem | | The Solution | |
|---|---|---|---|
| What is the problem? | | What is the solution? | |
| How does it affect people? | | How will it benefit people? | |
| What is the evidence? | | What is the evidence for the solutions? (include precedents) | |
| Outline a human example | | Who/what needs to change? | |
| Who is responsible? | | What action needs to be taken, and by whom? | |

## Campaigning and language 2 – framing the debate on the sexual abuse of children

At the beginning of Barnardo's campaigning on issues relating to the sexual abuse of children, there was recognition of the need to change the way that people talked about the issues. Barnardo's programme experience at the time was that even the police tended to treat the children as criminals rather than as vulnerable victims of abuse. In seeking to reframe the way in which the issue is perceived, Barnardo's campaigning has been consistent and tenacious in challenging the terminology 'child prostitutes', arguing that this legitimised what was going on by implying some kind of choice made by the children involved, and that this didn't make sense because children can't consent to their own abuse. Challenging the language was important because this informed the way that people thought about, and behaved in relation to, the children involved.

The campaign has been characterised by a lot of early thought and discussion about how best to talk about the issue and significant internal effort to ensure consistency of message – for example, through the production of a series of internal briefing papers and media training for those involved in the campaign.

Once you have framed the issue as you want it – in a paragraph or two – this can be circulated internally and also to your external 'friends' in the policy-making field.

Even though everyone has been involved in planning a campaign and agreeing solutions and strategy, at some point their memories of what was agreed can easily diverge. Organisations can spend ridiculous amounts of time revisiting old discussions with altered perceptions.

Having the framed issue statement on hand throughout the campaign prevents these disagreements because it is all there in black and white for everyone to see, and everyone has signed up to it.

Framing the issue in this way is also a useful foundation for developing messages targeted at specific audiences – which should all be derived from, and consistent with, the overall way that the campaign is being described.

Framing the issue also presents an opportunity to reference back. Does the aim need revising once you have considered the issue again? This is, of course, something that should be done throughout the campaign cycle to ensure that that everything you have done still holds good.

## 4.4 Identifying routes of influence

Now you need to draw up how you will achieve your campaign aim. In setting your aim, you should have identified the campaign target.

To identify the routes of influence, you need to answer the following questions:
- who is the campaign target (included in your aim)?
- how much influence do you and your allies have over the target?
- what and who influences the campaign target?
- what are the best ways for you to reach your target, directly and indirectly?

To exert influence on an institutional target successfully you need to understand what makes it 'tick' – its political dynamic. Within any institution, a complex web of internal and external pressures, competing demands and self-interest influences policies and practice. Make no mistake about it, policy change is political.

**If you do not understand what motivates or deters the key decision makers in regard to your issue, you restrict your chances of achieving positive change.**

If you do not understand what motivates or deters the key decision makers in regard to your issue, you restrict your chances of achieving positive change. This is where VCOs are often at their weakest; mistakenly assuming that because they occupy the moral high ground and can state their case eloquently, change will inevitably occur. If only politics were that simple.

Even if politicians know the detail of an issue, realise it is morally and practically sensible, and agree with the voluntary sector, they may still have absolutely no intention of taking any action in support of the campaign aim.

Often VCOs simply do not make it 'worth the politicians' while' – either positively (through feel-good or associated good publicity of backing a winner) or negatively (they hadn't proved they could create a nuisance at so many levels that the issue could not be ignored). At other times, the VCS case risks being so unspecific and muddled that it acts as a deterrent to politicians' involvement.

## A Labour MP's view

"They come to me with a good cause and of course it makes moral sense and of course I agree with it. But it's simply not practical in the current political context. It's useless expecting to get a result just because the message is morally right. We need to think politically – what does my party feel about it and what are the implications for me if I go against my party (especially if the campaign allies are political dynamite)? Does it fit into the legislative programme anywhere? Why should I bother when there are a hundred conflicting calls on my time?"

### 4.4.1 Steps to influencing policy makers

Understanding the policy-making process need not be daunting. It can be done simply and systematically:

1. Draw up an **influence map** showing who may have influence over how decisions about your issue will be made.
2. Create a **power analysis** chart identifying your allies and opponents and their relatives strengths.
3. Use the above to prioritise **influence routes** to reach the campaign target.

As well as longevity, another feature of successful campaigns is often serendipity. The momentum of the campaign against fox hunting for example was aided in 1997 when Mike Foster MP came first in the selection of Private Members' Bills and chose to introduce a Bill to ban fox hunting, partly as a result of consultation with his Worcester constituents, amongst whom there was a strong and well-organised League Against Cruel Sports local group. The MP was personally committed to a ban but the strength of feeling shown by constituents may have helped in the decision. Although his Bill failed to reach the statute book, it raised the profile of the issue, pushing it right up the political agenda, where it stayed.

### 4.4.2 Identifying who influences the target

So the first step is to try to work out who influences your target and how.

One way to do this is to draw up an **influence map**, identifying everyone who may affect the policy process related to this issue. For example, MPs can be influenced through other MPs, their constituencies, parliamentary groups, the corporate sector, family interests, employers in their constituencies etc. It helps at this stage to think laterally and involve a wide spectrum of people – sometimes the most unlikely of your staff/volunteers/clients may know people who play an influencing role. This is also the time to involve 'insiders' in the process. They will have valuable knowledge about the unofficial influence routes in the institution or to the individual you wish to reach. These may not be obvious from the outside but may provide shortcuts to the decision makers.

## Inside knowledge

To different observers the British Parliament will be seen to function in different ways. The public, watching the yah-boo antics of the House of Commons Chamber on TV, would be forgiven for thinking that change happens through verbal bun-fights, conquest being dependent on MPs' skills of rhetoric and showman-like debate. The campaigns staff of VCOs, in contrast, will often be obsessed with the 'official' version of how legislation is made and altered – the stages of Bills, the Standing Committees and procedures for Parliamentary Questions.

MPs operating in the thick of the political machine, however, will know that much of the real politics takes place away from the Chamber, through 'unofficial' routes that are rarely understood or even known about by VCOs yet could be highly beneficial to them. For example, most experienced campaigners know of the House of Commons official Select Committees which oversee the work of government departments. Few however, are aware of the Labour MPs' own Departmental Committees that meet regularly with Labour Ministers for frank and open debates and which are rarely approached by VCOs. Few are also aware of the MPs' Regional Groups, which can be extremely useful routes of influence to VCOs operating at local level. Within Parliament, there are continual informal lobbying meetings between MPs (especially government MPs) and Ministers and much of the 'real' politics in Parliament happens in the MPs-only tearoom or in the voting lobbies each day.

This type of inside knowledge of how Parliament works can be invaluable and applies equally to other campaign targets. All institutions have ways of working that may not be obvious to the outsider. VCOs should seek to involve insiders more at the planning stage of their campaigns to ensure any valuable unofficial influence routes are also built into the campaign strategy.

## National fire sprinkler campaign

The following example shows a simplified form of the influence tree that was compiled for the National Fire Sprinkler Campaign.

This campaign developed because it was not compulsory for superstores to fit fire sprinkler systems. If these enormous buildings were to catch fire, the blaze would spread rapidly, turning them into an inferno. Firefighters were put at risk and some killed having to enter these buildings, yet sprinkler systems would stop the blaze very quickly (there have been no fire deaths in sprinklered buildings to date). The Campaign wanted the Government to make sprinkler systems compulsory in all superstores over 2000m square but this was a complex task since responsibility was spread around several Government departments. The best option was to try to alter building regulations.

The influence tree identified several potential major influencers and assisted in creating a strong and unusual alliance between trades unions, the mass media, the insurance industry, responsible retailers and local authorities. After considerable work and consistent lobbying and communications, the law was changed to make sprinklers compulsory in 2000.

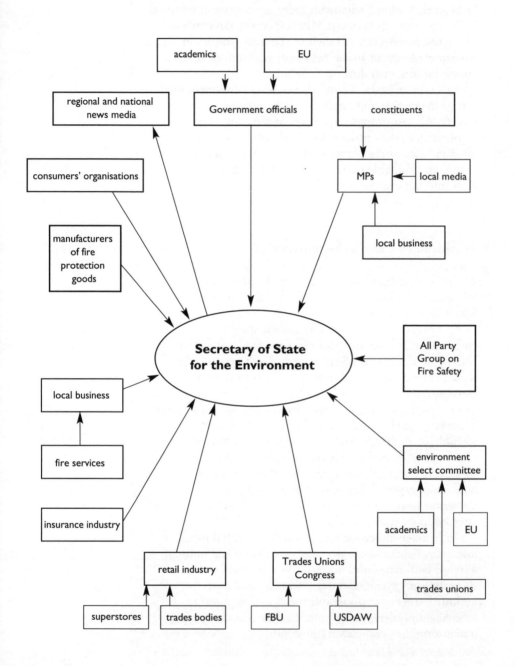

### 4.4.3 Defining where the power lies

Once you have identified all the possible influencers it is useful to see which of these can be recruited as allies and which are potential enemies. A power analysis is a good tool for this. Simply go through the influencers and divide them into known friends, foes or floaters (or allies, opponents and undecided).

| Friends | Floaters | Foes |
|---------|----------|------|
|         |          |      |

Your method of approach to friends, foes and floaters should vary. For friends you could involve them more, even in planning the campaign tactics. Do you have allies outside your sector (e.g. trades unions, corporate sector, academics)? Look for an alliance of the unexpected – this is often a powerful way to draw attention to your cause.

**Look for an alliance of the unexpected – this is often a powerful way to draw attention to your cause.**

---

## Building a campaign against the asylum voucher system

In its first term of office, Tony Blair's Labour Government decided to end monetary support for the families of asylum seekers and replace it with vouchers to be exchanged in designated shops. This was considered degrading and socially divisive by many VCOs and also MPs. As a result Oxfam, the Refugee Council and the Transport and General Workers Union (TGWU) forged an alliance to campaign against the new voucher system. The alliance was unusual, clearly not 'the usual suspects' and attracted the attention of MPs and officials. Bill Morris, then General Secretary of the TGWU championed the campaign in public at the TUC and in private with the Labour Party leadership. As a proxy advocate for the three organisations' campaign, he was a powerful influencer with access straight to the top of the Labour Government. The combination of an unusual, influential alliance, intense lobbying from the three organisations' supporters and pressure on the Minister from groups of MPs inside Parliament was successful. At the first politically acceptable opportunity (a new Home Secretary), the Government scrapped the asylum voucher system.

For foes, it is often best to try to isolate them totally and not provide them with ammunition that can be turned against you. You need to consider how strong your opponents are, what access to decision makers they have and whether you can act to neutralise that access or minimise the threat they hold.

Floaters need to be cajoled and persuaded of the justness of your cause. Often these people are the key to achieving change as they are susceptible to a well-made case and may change their perceptions. It is therefore wise to invest time and money in building their trust.

Of course, it makes sense to focus your efforts on the most important members of each of these categories. Ranking them according to their (actual or potential) influence may help in thinking about where best to dedicate effort and resources.

### 4.4.4 Influencing the influencers

Once you have an idea of where the power lies and who your allies may be you can look at how best to access them. Revisit the influence map and identify priority routes of influence on which your campaign is going to focus. This way, the influence map will help direct your efforts through the most appropriate channels to the key target.

For some key influencers the routes will be straightforward and you can access them directly. For others, you may need to go through several stages of secondary influences to reach them. For example, a key influencer may be the chairperson of a parliamentary committee with whom you have already had past dealings. In this case, you can contact her/him direct. If a key influencer however is a body with which you have no contacts, take for example the CBI, you may need to go through a secondary influence route – for example a member body such as a trades organisation. Or you may wish to exert influence via a major trades union but find you cannot get access to the top easily. In this case, you may need to work through the trades unions' regional structure or conference system.

Prioritising channels of influence helps you maximise the levers of power you have identified and makes strategic use of your limited resources.

It is worth being clear about which routes you intend to use as early on in the campaign as possible since some may require lengthy timescales, which you need to factor in when developing your strategy.

## A strategy format

You have now defined your campaign aim and developed your strategy. It may be useful to write the strategy down at this stage; this might incorporate:

- the rationale for the issue selected
- your campaign aim
- your framing statement
- identification of routes of influence, if necessary with background explanation.

But a strategy is not a plan; a strategy defines your broad approach but does not indicate how you will act to achieve your aim. That is the next part of the cycle.

## Learning point

You may wish to consider the following:

✓ Developing a strategy enables you to focus on how to achieve maximum impact for minimum investment.

✓ Is your campaign aim clear and specific?

✓ Consider how your campaign is framed by others – including opponents – and frame or reframe the issue to suit your interests.

✓ Do you understand the policy making process? Draw up an influence map, create a power analysis chart and prioritise influence routes.

✓ Does your strategy document incorporate rationale, campaign aim, framing statement and identification of routes of influence?

1. Hubert, D (2000) *The Landmine Ban: A Case Study for Humanitarian Advocacy*. The Thomas J Watson Jr Institute for International Studies
2. Cohen, D, de la Vega, R and Watson, G (2001) *Advocacy for Social Justice: A Global Action and Reflection Guide*. Kumarian Press Inc. and Vaneklasen, L with Miller, V (2002) *A new weave of power, people and politics: The action guide for advocacy & citizen participation*. World Neighbors

# 5 Setting objectives and action planning

*"Everything should be made as simple as possible, but not simpler."*
**Albert Einstein**

## 5.1 Setting clear measurable objectives

An aim gives you an idea of where you are going; it identifies what the campaign is designed to achieve.

A strategy gives you an idea of the most effective routes to get there.

Campaign objectives guide you along a path towards your final aim. They make explicit your thinking about how the aim will be reached.

Identifying the milestones of change – the campaign objectives – will help you focus and coordinate your campaigning effort to achieve maximum impact.

Think back to the impact chain. You will have set a campaign aim in the belief that, if you achieve it, positive change in people's lives will result. In almost all cases, there will be a series of short, medium and possibly longer-term outcomes that you will seek to achieve that lead to the achievement of this aim. Making these explicit by codifying them into objectives will:

- help you target campaigning effort and
- give you a yardstick against which to assess your progress.

To fulfil both of these criteria, and for objectives to be most useful, you need to be able to tell whether they have been achieved or not. In other words, they need to be measurable.

Best practice therefore suggests that objectives should ideally:

- identify a **specific target** or target group (who is going to change?)
- define a **specific change** (what will they know, or think or do that is different?)
- stipulate the **timeframe of change** (when will it happen by?)

For objectives to be most useful, you need to be able to tell whether they have been achieved or not. In other words, they need to be measurable.

**Be prepared to adapt your objectives as the campaign develops.**

## SMART objectives?

In relation to objectives, the acronym SMART has come into common usage. It is usually taken to mean that objectives should be specific, measurable, achievable, realistic, timetabled. But, beware; there is a danger that the SMART model has become overused. It has become so devalued that it actively discourages people from thinking through objectives, as it has become simply a process of ticking boxes (which people may not see the point of) rather than a useful tool for thinking through choices. The point is to set useful objectives, not slavishly to adopt an acronym.

But, of course, campaigns do not usually progress along a set of straight and clear paths so you need to be flexible: be prepared to adapt your objectives as the campaign develops.

Objectives should be a tool not a straightjacket.

**Your objectives should primarily be measuring your progress towards the aim, not measuring how busy you are.**

## Objectives, outputs, outcomes, impact

In Part One the impact chain was introduced, stressing the importance of distinguishing between levels of change, noting that impact relates to actual change in people's lives, that outcomes are the effects of a particular intervention, and that outputs are a measure of effort. To reiterate here what was suggested then: "Getting stuck at thinking about outputs means concentrating on effort. Effort is important but it must be focused to be effective. Focusing your attention on the effects of your efforts – the outcomes – should help you think about how effective you are being, and, ultimately, whether your campaigning is making an impact."

This is key when setting objectives. Your objectives should primarily be measuring your progress towards the aim, not measuring how busy you are.

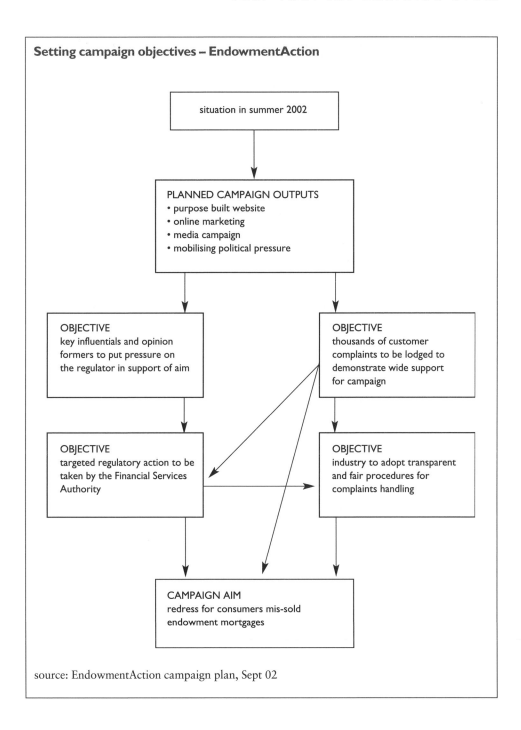

**Setting campaign objectives – EndowmentAction**

situation in summer 2002

PLANNED CAMPAIGN OUTPUTS
• purpose built website
• online marketing
• media campaign
• mobilising political pressure

OBJECTIVE
key influentials and opinion formers to put pressure on the regulator in support of aim

OBJECTIVE
thousands of customer complaints to be lodged to demonstrate wide support for campaign

OBJECTIVE
targeted regulatory action to be taken by the Financial Services Authority

OBJECTIVE
industry to adopt transparent and fair procedures for complaints handling

CAMPAIGN AIM
redress for consumers mis-sold endowment mortgages

source: EndowmentAction campaign plan, Sept 02

The diagram (previous page) represents a summary of the objectives originally set for the Consumers Association [now Which?] campaign on endowment mis-selling, launched in September 2002. The arrows show how it was planned that the campaign would progress towards its aim. This shows the logic behind the campaign and is an example of how campaign objectives can be either sequential (i.e. the achievement of one feeds into the next) and/or simultaneous (i.e. pursued in parallel).

An early evaluation of the campaign showed that progress had already been made towards achieving these objectives, for example that:

- there had been nearly half a million visits to the endowmentaction.co.uk website;
- over 30,000 people had used the tools on the website to register a complaint with their mortgage provider;
- overall the rate of complaints to the Financial Services Authority [FSA] regarding mis-selling had more than doubled in the period since the campaign launch;
- there were early signs of movement within the FSA towards taking on an enhanced regulatory role.

The evaluation report concluded: "Establishing a campaign team with a coordinator and a full and detailed campaign plan, with agreed objectives, audiences, activities and key messages was one of the main reasons why the campaign has operated so smoothly."

[from EndowmentAction Interim Campaign Evaluation, March 2003, by Louise Hanson, Marina Cheal & Miranda Watson, quoted with permission]

## 5.2 Establishing the monitoring and evaluation framework

**A time and place for monitoring and evaluation**

Monitoring and evaluation are introduced at this point in the cycle because it is important to think about these essential parts of any campaign at the beginning of your campaign, not just at the end. Monitoring should be about tracking progress towards your objectives. Evaluation is about assessing that progress at essential points in the campaign. That's why it makes sense to get the framework in place at the same time as you are setting your objectives.

*Monitoring should be about tracking progress towards your objectives. Evaluation is about assessing that progress at essential points in the campaign.*

Monitoring asks, 'How is the campaign doing?' – a question that should be asked throughout the duration of the campaign. This enables you to identify what is working and what isn't working so well. Doing this on an ongoing basis allows you to adapt strategy and tactics.

Evaluation looks back to make judgements about past effectiveness – 'Did the campaign achieve its aim?'. It also looks forward and by learning from experience is used to improve future practice – 'What lessons can be learned?'. Evaluations are snapshots occurring at fixed times (see section 7 for a notional timetable) that create space for reflection and learning.

What distinguishes monitoring and evaluation are the questions being asked and the time at which they are asked. The techniques of answering them are broadly interchangeable and it makes sense to create a single framework for monitoring and evaluation, rather than thinking of them as separate functions.

It is likely that you will want to explore questions around both progress and process. You will be testing the validity of the assumptions you have developed in your strategy about how change in this context is likely to happen and how you can best mobilise your resources to effect it.

In summary, this means that any framework should ideally address the following questions:

**Key questions in monitoring and evaluation**

| | |
|---|---|
| **INPUTS/ ACTIVITIES** | • Can financial accountability be demonstrated?<br>• Have activities been delivered according to plan? If not, what accounts for any discrepancy?<br>• Is the campaign management appropriate?<br>• Has the process of campaigning been a positive one? |
| **OUTPUTS** | • Have the range of outputs been delivered according to the plan? If not, what accounts for any discrepancy? |
| **OUTCOMES** | • How much progress has been made towards the campaign's objectives?<br>• What other factors are contributing to or impeding achievement of the objectives?<br>• To what extent are the objectives contributing to progress towards the aim? |
| **IMPACT** | • What changes in people's lives have resulted from, or been influenced by, the campaign?<br>• To what extent does the campaign appear to be moving towards having positive impact? |

**Measuring outcomes and assessing impact should be the focus of monitoring and evaluation.**

Measuring outcomes and assessing impact should be the focus of monitoring and evaluation. This is because:

- this kind of scrutiny helps focus on the core purpose of **effecting change**
- this is a vital component of organisational **accountability**, i.e. it's a way of investigating whether resources invested in campaigning are being productively used
- this approach forms a basis for making **strategic judgements** about future campaigning directions
- demonstrating progress (as well as showing you are prepared to learn from mistakes) can be **motivating** for staff, volunteers, supporters, beneficiaries
- **what gets measured gets done** – that is why it is important that the objectives are thought through and clearly linked to the achievement of the campaign aim.

### 5.2.1 Objectives, indicators and means of verification

Assessing campaigns is about building the evidence so that you can make a reasoned case that your intervention has contributed towards change – or not.

In almost every situation, it will almost certainly not be possible to establish a direct causal link between your campaign and any changes that occur in relation to the issue you are campaigning on. That is why it is unwise to spend time looking for this kind of proof. Social and political change is complex, and depends on many variables. For this reason, best practice indicates that the various techniques used in campaign evaluation (and outlined in Section 11) would normally be used in combination, to build a 'critical mass' of evidence. How you do this depends on the scale, scope and nature of the specific campaign.

However, whatever the issue, there is at least one constant – that monitoring and evaluation should be about measuring progress towards the campaign aim, through the achievement of your objectives.

This means that, once campaign objectives have been identified, two questions can be asked against each:

- what are the indicators of progress – what key pieces of evidence will show whether a particular objective is being met, or not?
- what are the means of verification – which sources will you go to and which techniques will you use to gather this evidence?

**Relationship between objectives, indicators and means of verification**

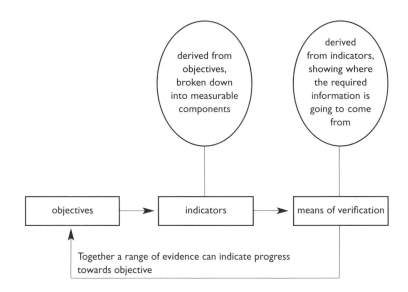

| objectives | | indicators | | means of verification |

derived from objectives, broken down into measurable components

derived from indicators, showing where the required information is going to come from

Together a range of evidence can indicate progress towards objective

### 5.2.2 Indicators

When thinking about what evidence to focus on in measuring progress towards objectives, it may be helpful to bear in mind that the best indicators are:
- measurable – i.e. it needs to be reasonably clear whether they have been achieved or not
- representative – i.e. they should cover the most important aspects of the objective; sometimes this will require a set of indicators rather than just one
- reliable – meaning not only that they can be measured in a standard way, but that the relationship between the indicator and the objective needs to be clear
- feasible – so that information can be gathered at reasonable cost and effort; this will vary according to the size and scope of the campaign and its resources.

### 5.2.3 Means of verification

When thinking about the best ways of gathering the information you require, best practice suggests that:
- where possible, you should make sure you build in an opportunity to cross-check evidence from different sources
- in particular, you should try and include a mix of quantitative (statistical) data and qualitative information (derived from interviews for example and representing people's perceptions of the campaign).

When identifying the means of verification, it is important to make clear too how (and when) relevant information will be gathered. Not only this, you should consider how and when the information will be stored, and how and when it will actually be used.

---

**To take a composite example of a campaign aimed at influencing an institution (such as a financial institution) through engagement and lobbying:**

the campaign **objectives** might be to achieve:
- demonstrably raised awareness amongst policy makers of the issue;
- demonstrably enhanced willingness of policy makers to engage in a debate on the issue;

---

- the securing within x years agreement from policy makers to consider effecting changes in policy and/or practice;
- an introduction within y years change in institutional policy and/or practice in line with the campaign aim.

In which case **indicators of progress** identified might include evidence relating to changes over time in the following:
- the amount of attention paid to the issue by policy makers;
- the language used by policy makers to describe the issue;
- policy makers' willingness to meet, and the delay or speed in establishing a meeting date;
- the status of those attending any meeting;
- the level of trust shown within meetings, as evinced for example by sharing of documents and information;
- the level of confidence shown in the organisation's knowledge and capacity, as shown for example by requests for information and advice;
- how meetings are documented, for example whether they conclude with action points
- the willingness to continue – and formalise – a meeting process;[2]
- the degree and precision to which policy makers are prepared to make a commitment to address the issue along the lines promoted in the campaign;
- evidence of any changes in policy and practice introduced or being considered.

in which case, some of the possible **means of verification** might include:
- collecting evidence – for example from policy statements, correspondence, etc – of shifting policy positions or signs of enhanced support;
- periodic self-assessment (backed where possible by documentary evidence) of how the campaign is progressing towards its objectives, for example how relationships with policy makers are developing;
- gathering some impressions of the campaign and its effects from within the target institution, for example by commissioning an external evaluator to conduct interviews with policy makers and officials;

- gathering contributions through interviews and other inputs from others with an interest in the campaign, such as allies within the network, MPs on the relevant Select Committee, etc;
- feedback from intended beneficiaries on the extent to which their voices and aspirations are heard within the campaign.

## 5.3 Developing workplans

Having set objectives, the next stage is to develop workplans to show how activity will be managed to achieve the objectives.

Workplanning involves:
- identifying the tasks that are necessary to deliver the objectives
- ensuring that the resources are available for and assigned to the tasks
- timetabling the tasks.

A workplan details what people are going to do to achieve the objectives (and hence the aim).

Given the complexities of campaigning, especially in larger organisations, there are many advantages to having a written workplan. The key ones are that workplans:
- make it easier for people to be clear what needs to be done and what lies within their personal area of responsibility
- can help develop understanding of campaigning
- are a tool for getting organisational agreement to the campaign
- help ensure that appropriate resources are allocated to tasks
- help in monitoring progress
- provide a record of intentions against which a campaign can be evaluated.

But these benefits have to be traded against the fact that work-planning can be time consuming and that the campaign context is liable to change, making detailed plans redundant.

The important thing is that those working on the campaign are, together, delivering a coherent approach. To secure that, in some circumstances (where, for example, a small number of experienced campaigners are working closely together) it will be enough to have common agreement about the key objectives and broad strategy. In other circumstances (for example, in larger organisations where campaign delivery involves different departments) it may well be necessary to plan in greater detail.

Many organisations will now have agreed project management systems in place and many will use a performance management and appraisal system. A campaign plan should link to these. Workplanning can be used to reconcile campaign objectives to personal objectives and then with organisational objectives. So the individual campaigners have personal objectives that if achieved lead to the achievement of the campaign's objectives and these will in turn lead to the achievement of the organisation's objectives.

If your organisation plans on an annual cycle it may make sense to integrate the campaign planning process into this process. But be careful: planning a campaign a year in advance may prove problematic because it is difficult see that far ahead with accuracy. One approach would be to determine a clear sense of activities and priorities over a 3-6 month period, updated on a rolling basis but within a broader framework looking a year or more ahead.

**Workplanning can be used to reconcile campaign objectives to personal objectives and then with organisational objectives.**

## Forward planning

The Child Poverty Action Group, for example, plans on the basis of a forward grid (see below), starting from an external perspective and building a plan around known events in the public arena, looking up to 18 months ahead. Taking external events and hooks as the starting point, planning then involves looking at how internal campaign activity can best fit with, and exploit the opportunities of, these external deadlines and timetables:

| Month | External events & hooks | Policy submissions | Publications | Events and launches | Web | Press | Mailings |
|-------|-------------------------|--------------------|--------------|---------------------|-----|-------|----------|
|       |                         |                    |              |                     |     |       |          |
|       |                         |                    |              |                     |     |       |          |
|       |                         |                    |              |                     |     |       |          |
|       |                         |                    |              |                     |     |       |          |
|       |                         |                    |              |                     |     |       |          |

Similarly, the NSPCC plans up to 18 months ahead, identifying anticipated lead issues over such a period, although recognising of course that the situation can change. Planning is more detailed towards the deadline, but even then plans are based on the acknowledgement that the NSPCC is not in complete control of the campaigning agenda and that there may need to be space created to react to issues that arise in the public domain.

## Campaign timeline

Too many VCOs set arbitrary internal timescales for their campaigns without due reference to the external climate in which they are working.

It is amazing how many VCOs run two-year campaigns then promptly pull the plug on all activity. Most campaigns will need to be sustained beyond internal time constraints – sometimes you will need to be committed to a long haul.

### Don't pull the plug too soon – social change takes time

One analysis is that part of the success of the campaign to ban fox hunting goes back to the early 1980s when one focus of the campaign was to get local county councils to ban hunting on their land. This tactic was not a long term success – the approach was declared illegal after a few years – but it meant that generations of Labour Party activists and councillors came into contact with, and pledged support for, the issue. Many involved in this way subsequently became MPs, particularly in the 1997 intake, and were willing to follow up the idea of banning hunting in their new roles.

Based on external analysis you will know the important dates and timetable for those you are influencing. This, rather than internal desire, should be the timelines you work to for your campaign. As well as an overall timeline, you should have timelines for each audience and set of activities and be careful to build in a sensible amount of time for the inevitable slippage that always occurs and throws everyone into a spin.

## 5.4 Testing the plan

One ultimate virtue of workplanning is that it gives you one final opportunity to test the plan and the thinking on which it is based: Is it robust? Is it achievable? Is it coherent?

---

**The kinds of questions you should ask in revisiting your plan are:**

aim
- does the campaign aim succinctly express what the campaign will achieve?
- is it inspiring? (if you're not inspired by it, who else will be?)
- does it identify who needs to change, and how they should change in order for the campaign to be successful?
- can you say with reasonable certainty that achieving this aim will have a positive impact on people's lives?
- is there a commitment to keep campaigning until the goal is achieved? If not, what is the alternative exit strategy?

outcomes
- is it clear that the objectives you have identified are necessary in order to achieve the aim?
- do they make clear the change that needs to happen – for example in public behaviour and/or institutional policy and practice?
- are they measurable?
- are they realistic given the time and resources available?
- is it clear that the organisation is in a position to generate the effort (the outputs) required to contribute to their achievement?
- are systems to monitor and evaluate progress in place?

outputs
- is it clear that activities you are in a position to be able to organise will contribute to the achievement of these outputs?
- do they describe together a set of achievements that are needed to achieve the outcomes you have identified?
- is there a set of practical actions to achieve each output?
- are systems in place to ensure efficient use of resources?

---

**activities**
- are the major activities listed? are they coherent? are they necessary?
- is the list manageable?
- do they reflect main actions required to achieve the outputs?
- are resources identified that will help you deliver these activities?
- are these resources sufficient?[3]

This testing of the plan should occur not just at the end of the first planning phase. It's important to keep revisiting the approach, and checking the assumptions behind, and the progress of, the campaign at periods throughout the campaign's duration (see evaluation timetable, Section 7).

The point is that you should be on top of the progress of the campaign and be in a position to adapt strategy and tactics accordingly.

Where progress towards objectives diverges from expectations, in managing the ongoing campaign you have three choices:
- change tactics so that you can secure the objective through a different route
- revise the objectives, for example by extending the timetable within which you expect change to take place, or if you suspect that your efforts could more usefully be focused in a different direction
- continue unchanged, if, for example, your assessment is that existing hurdles or delays are likely to be overcome further on in the campaign

### The campaign control loop

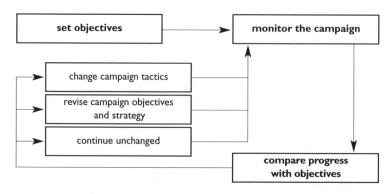

## 5.5 Contingency planning

The trick in campaigning is not so much to plan things, as to plan for things.

**The trick in campaigning is not so much to plan things, as to plan for things.**

As the German military found out in 1914, it was all very well for them to have the elaborately developed Schlieffen Plan up their sleeves, but within a few days of the outbreak of the First World War, the whole plan was in tatters. Von Schlieffen, the author of the plan, had anticipated that initially the war would take place on the Western Front only and therefore failed to factor in the prospect that Russia would mobilise its army in support of Serbian nationalism after the assassination of Franz Ferdinand. Von Schlieffen also underestimated the response of the Belgian and British armies. As a result, instead of overrunning France within six weeks, the German troops got only as far as Flanders.

To avoid making the same kind of mistake, when launching a campaign, and at key points in its development, it may be a good idea to consider what kinds of reactions the campaign might engender, from the target and other key players, and to explore the implications of these and how the campaign, in turn, should react.

In thinking about how the target will react, it might help to plot various scenarios and explore their implications.

---

**Responsive campaigning**

One way to react to different audiences' responses to your campaign issues is to categorise their response and develop reaction accordingly:
- are they receptive?
- have they misunderstood, or failed to be convinced by your arguments?
- have they understood your arguments, but rejected them?

In each case, in your developing campaign, you could consider:
- what are they likely to do as a result?
- what opportunity and/or threat does this create for the campaign?
- how should strategy and tactics be adapted accordingly?

---

The principle is to be prepared. A contingency plan should demonstrate that your organisation has thought through possible reactions to the campaign and is flexible enough to respond appropriately.

---

**A plan format**

The following structure may be helpful when drawing up a campaign plan. The point is that the plan should summarise your thinking and planned activity so that there is a common understanding of the campaign.
- brief background context
- statement of campaign aim
- objectives
- monitoring and evaluation framework
- workplans – schedule of work, matching activities to each objective
- identification of resources required – staff and budget
- contingency plans
- timeline

---

## Learning points

You may wish to consider the following:
- ✓ Planning is important in ensuring that those working on the campaign are, together, delivering a coherent approach.
- ✓ Are your objectives clear and measurable and do they identify a specific target, define a specific change and stipulate the timeframe of change?
- ✓ Are your indicators (which measure progress towards objectives) measurable, representative, reliable and feasible?
- ✓ What are your means of verification – does it make it clear how information will be gathered; how and when it will be stored; and, how and when it will be used?
- ✓ Does your workplan identify tasks, ensure resources are available and assigned and provide a timetable?
- ✓ Have you tested your workplan: is it robust, achievable and coherent?

1. International Fund for Agriculture Development (2002) *Managing for Impact in Rural Development: A Guide for Project M&E*. IFAD

2. Davies, R (2001) *Evaluating the Effectiveness of DFID's Influence with Multilaterals: Part A, A Review of NGO Approaches to Evaluation of Advocacy Work*. DFID

3. See 1. above, and WK Kellogg Foundation (2001) *Logical Model Development Guide*. WK Kellogg Foundation

# 6 Delivering the campaign

"Jumble sales are organised and pamphlets have been posted
Even after closing time there's still parties to be hosted
You can be active with the activists
Or sleep in with the sleepers
While you're waiting for the Great Leap Forwards."
**Billy Bragg, Waiting For The Great Leap Forward**

## 6.1 Look before you leap

Some readers will have skipped to this bit. Most campaigners want to get on with it and think campaigning is about action – doing things.

It is. But being busy is not in itself a virtue. Action should be prized only if it is clearly focused on achieving your aim. The most effective campaigns are meticulously planned before being carefully executed.

At this stage, you should have a clear aim and objectives. You know who your main target is and what your routes of influence are going to be. Now you need to get your message across to those who matter – working through your identified influence routes to reach your target, preferably from as many sides as possible.

The best campaigns have a clearly defined aim that can be achieved by mixing the right ingredients – a bit like a recipe. It is helpful to look at this process as a series of steps:

1. understanding your audiences
2. pitching the message
3. identifying the campaign mix
4. developing campaign actions
5. communicating with your audiences

**The best campaigns have a clearly defined aim that can be achieved by mixing the right ingredients**

## 6.2 Understanding your audiences

The idea that, for any campaign, the target audience could be the 'general public' never stands up to scrutiny. With limited resources, it makes no sense to aim this widely. Even in situations where mass public support is needed, it's not possible to generate the amount of campaign coverage that would be needed to access all audiences within the general public.

Failing to segment and target audiences beyond the 'general public' is likely to represent an inefficient use of resources, a scattergun approach that those promoting messages for profit, for example through advertising, would never resort to. Even the Coca Cola Corporation doesn't proclaim its target audience to be the population of the world, as one campaign we evaluated defined its target audience.

Segmentation and targeting strategies adopted by corporate marketing tend to be underpinned by variables such as demographics (age, occupation, education, etc.) or psychographics (lifestyle, interests, etc.). Another way to categorise your audiences is to follow a conventional marketing typology of social class (A, B, C1 and C2, D, E).

Applying segmentation to a campaign-specific context means looking at how audiences are likely to engage at different levels. One simple way to do this is to distinguish between the following audiences:

1. political, administrative and communications elites
2. politically interested audiences (in most cases can be roughly equated with broadsheet readership)
3. mass audiences (roughly equated with tabloid readership)

Many campaigns revolve around trying to influence mass audiences, and sometimes find a convenient target audience in the readership of the tabloids – usually *The Sun* and *The Mirror* (the 'redtops') or the *Mail* and the *Express* (the 'bluetops'). If these papers take up your cause it tends to be perceived that you have achieved real impact and that the powers that be will sit up and take notice of you. In some cases, obviously, this will make sense; but success is by no means guaranteed and energy can be wasted by pursuing these audiences unstrategically.

For a start, "the majority of issues … are of such a technical character that there is no public opinion in relation to them".[1] And where there is significant public opinion on an issue, it may well be less sympathetic and more entrenched than the opinion and stance of the political elites.

> **Failing to segment and target audiences beyond the 'general public' is likely to represent an inefficient use of resources.**

What should be done in those circumstances? Does it make sense to devote campaign resources to trying to bring the tabloids' editorial position more in line with your perspective on the issue? In some instances it may do, but only if timescales allow. With limited resources – and especially in limited timescales – it is very difficult to make headway in these kinds of contexts. Even with astute nurturing of tabloid journalists, it takes a lot of time; more time than tends to be allocated to the typical campaign.

## Landmines campaign

When popular campaigning reaches a wide audience it can work well but, in the end, success at this level is usually outside the control of most campaigners. The publicity generated by the decision of Diana, Princess of Wales, to support the landmines campaign undoubtedly helped embed the campaign in the popular consciousness. But planning for such an intervention and devoting significant resources to securing the support of such high-profile figures is a risky strategy. The involvement of the Princess of Wales was preceded by a period of campaigning for a UK ban on landmines. This campaign utilised a wide range of public figures and careful nurturing of opposition politicians in the Labour Party who were likely to be elected to Government in the UK in 1997.

The fact that the incoming Government was pledged to signing up to the international treaty introducing the ban on landmines – when combined with the publicity generated by the support of the Princess of Wales – produced a set of unusual circumstances. The point is that the campaign did make plans to widen support for the ban (Princess Diana became involved as a patron of the Red Cross), to generate public concern (tabloids had covered the issue when other public figures had supported it) and to target decision makers (through careful targeting of MPs through constituents). What it didn't plan for was a set of circumstances that brought all these together in such a spectacular fashion.

Even in situations where it makes sense to target wider audiences, the concept of mass audience can itself sensibly be sub-divided. A simple approach to audience segmentation would:
1. take into account the spectrum of responses to a particular issue, ranging from supportive to hostile; and, as a result

2. identify different audience segments; and then
3. target different messages at them.

### 6.2.1 Pitching the message

So it is worth spending a little time thinking through what kind of people your audiences are and asking yourselves some important questions about how they access information before deciding how to communicate with them.

There is a need to attempt to get inside their minds and understand their lifestyles. Their lifestyles (for example, how busy they are, what circles they move in, their personal interests) will affect how they access information and the kinds of messages that resonate with them. There are several ways of making sense of this graphically. One technique used by marketing agencies to understand their customers is to carry out a paper 'role play' for the key audiences. Think creatively and imagine how that person gets their information, what they like to read, see or hear, what their interests are then attempt to depict this on paper graphically.

---

### Understanding the audiences: The Local Food in Local Supermarkets Campaign

A Local Food Campaign Team carried out a role-play exercise to try to understand the communications needs of three key audiences who would act as influencers on the Minster for Consumer Affairs. Using their influence map and experience of interviewing real-life people, they created three fictional characters who would exemplify the key audiences. They imagined what these individuals were like, where they obtained their information and what their media tastes could be and used them when planning communications throughout the campaign.

Mr Khan is a senior government official in the Department of Trade and Industry. He receives his information from trade press, conferences, business sections of broadsheet newspapers, detailed academic reports and the internet. For his work, he prefers specialist information with lots of facts, statistics and models. He finds examples of good practice from local authorities compelling and heeds warnings of problems from in-house gossip columns. He can accept complex campaign demands.

---

Mrs Jones is a consumer and loyal shopper with a major supermarket chain. She gets her information from tabloid newspapers, especially the 'blue tops' (*Daily Mail* and *Daily Express*); she listens to radio (Classic FM and the BBC local station) and buys glossy gardening and food magazines. She relates to human-interest stories, graphic descriptions and emotionally compelling messages. She is busy with young children at home and a part-time job so appreciates simple, practical campaign demands.

Angela Whiting is a farmer and fresh fruit producer unable to get her produce into the supermarkets. She is an astute businesswoman who gets her information from TV, the farming press and local newspapers as well as from mailings and briefings from farmers' organisations. She rarely gets time to read anything at length so needs catchy, compelling visuals and articles containing information suited to her situation. This issue affects her livelihood so she wants the details and can respond to relatively complex campaign demands.

The campaign team kept these three characters in mind when deciding on tactics, messages and materials for their campaign. As the campaign develops, these characters will be revisited and new characters added if required.

Different messages should be pitched at different audiences. All messages should of course be developed from a common core message (identified in framing the campaign, Section 4). Specific pitches tailoring this core message to identified audiences should be based on an assessment of:

- what will be most persuasive for that audience
- what information it needs to hear
- what action you want that audience to take[2]

This analysis should guide message content, form, length and medium and the messenger.

It's clear that different audiences need varying levels of complexity and technical detail in the information they are sent. This may seem obvious but is often not properly taken into account when devising campaign materials and selecting communications channels. The 'pitch' appropriate for your identified audiences varies depending on how detailed and complex they wish or are able to receive messages and can be illustrated in the diagram overleaf[3]:

**Different audiences need varying levels of complexity and technical detail in the information they are sent.**

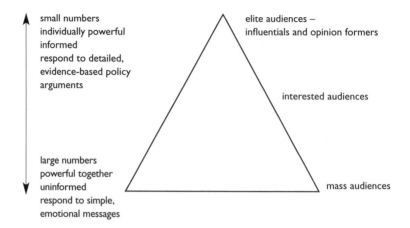

## 6.3 Identifying the campaign mix

In developing the campaign mix of approach and actions, for each audience you will need to select a mix of tactics that matches that audience's profile. When planning your activities do not see them in isolation. Think of it like an orchestra – the actions must sit comfortably together and resonate. Remember to focus on the outcomes.

A campaign usually has some or all of the following components:

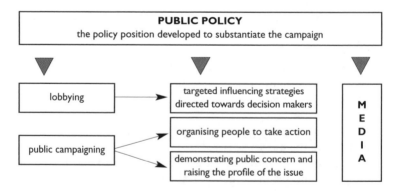

typology of campaigning
- lobbying – meetings, briefings, consultations
- public campaigning – organising people to take action through constituency visits, letters, postcards, public meetings

### 6.3.1 Lobbying

In the first instance, it is usually wise to consider a direct lobbying route. This is not just due to it being relatively benign in terms of budget and resources but also it helps gather information about how any public campaign will be received if the direct route fails. Targets will reveal their position in response to your direct contact that can then be used to develop appropriate tactics for public campaigning.

**Direct lobbying** entails a voluntary organisation developing contact directly with key targets (usually senior Government officials or Ministers or top company executives, etc.). This work tends to relay highly technical information, usually from a voluntary organisation's senior policy staff or directors.

Remember that most politicians in democratic systems want to win elections; indeed, in the western world, some argue that this has become the sole purpose of politicians. If this is the case, you have to convince them that if they accept your aim it will help them be elected. You may be more comfortable on the moral high ground, and there may be no shared agenda, but look at this first.

If direct lobbying appears to be making little progress (and beware of being 'captured' by the institution concerned and drawn into lengthy discourse that simply represents delaying and avoidance tactics) you can move onto indirect lobbying.

---

### The Parliamentary Event

You are holding a film showing for MPs, Lords and parliamentary staff. Rather than letting the audience 'escape' after the event, arrange for them to sign a visitors' book on entering. When they leave give them material with a simple direct campaign 'ask' and request they return it when the task is completed. If you do not hear from them use the information in the visitor's book to write to them or call them asking how best you can follow up with them.

---

**Indirect lobbying** activity involves mobilising other actors to pressurise important influencers, using your routes of influence, e.g. using the influential supporters or the public to pressurise Ministers. For instance, indirect lobbying also includes the use of MPs themselves to lobby their peers and Ministers.

Just as you should segment your target audience, it is also good practice to segment your supporters.

**Boomerang model**[4]

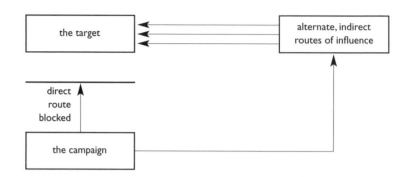

If you have supporters who ascribe to your campaign aim, think about how best to mobilise them. Some will be committed campaigners who expect to be asked to turn up to demonstrations: others may be suspicious of 'political' activity so you may wish to ask them to carry out a simple action like tell you that they support the campaign. You can then use their support for the campaign as part of actions. Just as you should segment your target audience, it is also good practice to segment your supporters.

1. Some (likely to be a relatively small number) will be committed campaigners, **advocates** prepared to act as representatives of the campaign, by visiting their MP, for example, or recruiting and mobilising others.
2. A larger group may be classified as **supporters**, keen to be informed about campaign developments and willing to take periodic action and/or donate in support of a specific campaign or the campaigning programme more generally.
3. Still others may be suspicious of 'political' activity or feel themselves to be too busy to take action, but may be willing to signal their support by, for example, taking some kind of symbolic action as **joiners**.

## The campaigners' trapezoid[5]

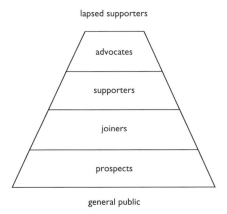

lapsed supporters

advocates

supporters

joiners

prospects

general public

---

### Managing a supporter base

The best supporter retention and development strategy allows for the maximising of each individual's level of support according to their specific needs, interests and desires. The level of sophistication at which it is possible for a supporter base to be segmented and managed will of course depend on resources, but ideally any approach should offer differentiated levels of information/requests for action, adapted to people's expressions of interest and levels of actual activity.

---

Remember that in a democracy constituents are particularly useful as they can persuade MPs to become interested in and act on an issue they would otherwise ignore. They can also be used to legitimise the interest of MPs who can raise an issue that they personally support but have no mandate to do so unless it is to represent the views of their constituents.

## The public meeting

Imagine you are holding a public meeting on the need for an integrated approach to domestic violence in Exeter. There are representatives present from the Police, education services, local councillors, domestic violence support organisations and community group leaders. They all participate and state their support. But what next? It is too easy for them to give public lip service on the day then go away with no intention of following up the issue (or be too busy to prioritise it). Instead, you could plan into the event a session where participants plan three steps for taking this forward in their own organisations. They can fill in two sections of a pledge card – one you keep and one they hold on to. This way they are 'pinned down' to follow up your campaign demands and have an incentive to prioritise it. This obviously has to be handled sensitively but it does demonstrate how a focus on outcomes not outputs can change the way you organise your campaign.

### 6.3.2 Public campaigning

Public campaigning can consume vast amounts of time and physical resources when compared to direct lobbying so if you have no pressing need to engage in public campaigning, don't.

## The demonstration

Is it enough to get 50,000 people to march through the streets if the decision makers are hidden way inside their buildings and do not notice? From our direct experience, it is quite possible to sit in Parliament with tens of thousands of demonstrators outside and not even know the event is happening! Far better to ensure that the demonstrators also lobby MPs in an organised manner on the day and that their details and the MPs' responses are recorded for future follow up.

**Just because you have lots of supporters who want to campaign doesn't mean to say that every campaign should involve public campaigning actions.**

Campaigning organisations sometimes seek to launch public campaigning without properly considering its purpose. Just because you have lots of supporters who want to campaign doesn't mean to say that every campaign should involve public campaigning actions like street stalls, demonstrations and other less legal forms of direct action. The latter has particularly problematic implications.

Greenpeace, for example, is very careful to ensure that the people who undertake the direct action which typifies its public profile are well trained and aware of the implications of taking part in the activities. It does not, as a rule, ask its supporters to undertake this type of activity.[6]

### 6.3.3 A note on direct action

In considering whether to take direct action, charities need to be careful about staying within the law and not offending key constituencies. There are of course many different forms of direct action, some of which are legal and respectable, some of which aren't.

### Types of direct action[7]

| form of action | purpose | legality |
|---|---|---|
| protest marches | demonstrate support/ levels of concern | usually legal |
| boycotts | inflict commercial sanction | legal |
| stunts | focus attention | may be marginally illegal |
| blockades, occupations | direct pressure | open to civil action, increasingly criminalised |
| destruction of property | intimidation, punishment | illegal |
| violence against individuals | | criminal |

## 6.4 Developing campaign actions

There is a vast range of campaign actions that you can utilise. Your choice will depend on:
- your audience
- your organisation's positioning
- your campaign approach.

Campaign actions have evolved dramatically over the past few years. There are numerous briefing papers, books and manuals explaining how to build websites, write press releases, organise events and lobby MPs (see the Bibliography for some useful resources). This book is not intended to repeat that work but to

The
campaign
airwaves are
crowded –
your message
needs to offer
something
different.

give you a structure for planning your campaigns and a methodology for approaching the options available.

There are, however, some points to be made about campaign actions in this context. For instance, it is important to realise that the campaign airwaves are crowded. Decision makers are constantly barraged with hundreds, if not thousands of competing messages each day and your message needs to offer something different, some 'extra value' to permeate all this white noise.

So when deciding on your portfolio of appropriate activities it may be worth inviting the relevant internal and external people (especially allies from inside the decision-making environment, e.g. a friendly MP or MP's assistant – there is always one somewhere – if not you're on to a loser!) to take part in a brainstorm.

## Maximising influence: four tools that campaigners have at their disposal[8]

- **Information politics** – getting reliable and pertinent information to key players in a format that is useful to them, and in a timely manner. Through the provision of policy papers to campaign targets VCOs can quickly become valued players in the political process.
- **Symbolic politics** – icons help to raise public awareness and generate public support. They attract attention and they engage emotions. They serve to represent complex issues, eventually becoming a code for easy and instant recognition of the issue. Symbolic politics are effective with the public, but also with decision makers who do not have time to delve deeply into complex issues. The wearing of badges or ribbons falls into this category.
- **Leverage politics** – where VCOs do not have easy access to decision makers, they may have access to other individuals who do. They must use leverage to utilise the connections they do have, to maximize the impact of their efforts – for instance by recruiting MPs to represent their cause in Parliament.
- **Accountability politics** – once authorities have made commitments to principle, VCOs are in a position to remind them through public encouragement or public admonition to keep to their word through encouraging the public to articulate their feelings in relation to their elected representatives by organising a lobby of Parliament.

There is a limited range of campaign actions and much energy has been spent looking for new ones. It is likely that any new action that you come up with will have been tried before. Don't worry. It does not matter if it is relatively new (text messaging) or as old as history (public meetings) – the question is what will be the outcome?

Of course, sometimes, doing the unexpected helps to get you noticed and get your issue up the political agenda – e.g. the 2001 fuel protests blockading fuel supplies to petrol stations was startlingly successful. But even with a tactic like this, once you (or someone else) have done something once a law of diminishing returns sets in. The same trick doesn't work so well twice, except maybe in a different context.

One of Saul Alinsky's rules for radicals is that, wherever possible your campaign should go outside of the experience of the target, and that once a tactic has been used it is no longer outside of their experience. For this reason, he suggests that one of the ideal characteristics of a campaign organiser is that they have the ability forever to create the new out of the old.

So, it is often a question of repackaging old ideas using a range of materials:

- Printed materials – reports, leaflets, postcards, bookmarks, posters, books, calendars, magazines, cartoon booklets, direct mail shots, magazine inserts, advertisements
- Videos, DVDs, films, CDs
- New media – emails, SMS texting, video-conferencing, campaign web pages, web networks
- Merchandise – branded T-shirts, mugs, badges, place mats and beer mats, telephone cards, pens, notepads, tax disc holders etc.
- Media coverage – national, regional and local newspapers and radio news items, features or comment slots, drama inclusions, TV regional and national news, features, comment slots, newspaper paid supplements, road shows, visits for decision makers to 'see for themselves'.

## Understanding the media

In its campaigning, Barnardo's has been keen to challenge media portrayal of children being sexually abused as 'child prostitutes'. In order to achieve this, aspects of working with the media over the years has included:
- dedicating significant time to discussing the issues with journalists so that they understood the importance of language
- keeping the language deliberately simple and repetitive, on the basis that if the message is too complex, it will inevitably get diluted
- supplying video images so that there were pictures for use that matched the reality of the situation that Barnardo's saw in its projects rather than the stereotypical images of child sex workers that the media otherwise tended to deploy.

Finding an original format, a snappy headline or an unexpected choice of messenger (a celebrity endorsement, a business executive, a well-known academic, or other states' leaders) can attract attention where otherwise you may be ignored. You are not just competing with other VCOs for air space with decision makers but also with a whole range of other advocates, for example:
- corporations – individually and as trade bodies
- individuals – MPs in particular now receive upwards of 200 letters a week from constituents and increasingly emails
- civil servants and the machinery of government who articulate and develop different policies all the time
- international institutions – the World Bank, UN, WTO all lobby decision makers
- professional lobby companies
- the media
- local authorities
- commissions, QUANGOS and other public bodies
- trades unions
- other campaigns

So how do you get targets to change? By shouting at them? Punishing them? Telling them they are evil? Or by persuading them that it is in their best interests to adopt the campaign demands? We have already seen that making a moral case is not enough.

You need to ensure that any message, however well supported, is credible and that practical solutions are available. Again, to quote Saul Alinsky: "The price of a successful attack is a constructive alternative."[9]

Politically the campaign has to either:

**Offer decision makers a win** from which they can bask in some reflected glory with their peers or their electorate. This may require offering levels of reassurance to decision makers who are naturally risk-averse. You can cite examples of where your demands have been carried out elsewhere (perhaps use case studies from other countries) with good results or perhaps produce a supporting line-up of the great and good, in particular experts and academics, to support your case.

**Persuade decision makers that your campaign demands are the lesser of two evils** and that if they ignore you the fallout could be politically damaging to them and their peers. For this a range of 'what if…' scenarios is useful. For example, if you do not install speed calming/road safety measures in X number of urban centres our campaign network will be collaborating with X academic institution to develop a monitoring system for all future accidents in those areas. Every year we will publish and publicise findings – the blame will come back very firmly and very publicly to the decision maker's doorstep.

One key decision is whether you need to concentrate all your communications efforts into a tight timespan (for example because of a looming legislation deadline) or whether you need to take a more subtle, longer-term approach. These choices can be summarised as representing two ends of a spectrum:

### (1) Saturation approach

This is where you attempt to 'blitz' your key targets with your campaign messages, hitting them from as many angles as possible within a short timescale. This is a useful approach when it is necessary to prove to opinion-formers that you have mass public support, especially if there is known opposition to your issue amongst decision makers.

The saturation approach is also useful to demonstrate to decision makers that your campaign has a high 'nuisance level'. There is such strength of feeling about the issue and you have so many routes of influence to access that there will be no foreseeable let up in your efforts over the medium term.

> The saturation approach is also useful to demonstrate to decision makers that your campaign has a high 'nuisance level'.

The decision makers then have to make a political judgement: can they ignore you and hope you will go away, or will the campaign noise simply climax, making the 'nuisance factor' too hard to ignore? In short, is it easier to deal with you now and offer concessions to your campaign demands – or risk having to concede even more later, with potentially damaging political backlash? From our direct experience within Parliament, these are the kinds of decisions made by MPs and Ministers every day.

### (2) Drip drip approach

**This may be more appropriate if the decision makers appear to be receptive to the campaign message but need gradual persuasion rather than full on hits.**

Rather than blitzing key targets with intense campaign messages, the 'drip drip' approach takes a more subtle, gradual approach to campaigning. This may be more appropriate if the decision makers appear to be receptive to the campaign message but need gradual persuasion rather than full on hits.

This approach can be punctuated with occasional intense periods of activity or events just to 'flex the campaigning muscles' and show decision makers that you are able to mobilise support and up the 'nuisance factor' if necessary. It puts the key targets on warning that a saturation campaign is highly likely if progress on campaign demands is not forthcoming within a reasonable timeframe.

Within your campaign strategy, you may decide to commence the campaign with a 'drip drip' approach for X number of months, moving to an intense 'saturation' campaign when certain trigger points of stalled progress occur.

Timing is crucial and there may well be times where you need to hold back. Attempting to force a political party to take a stance on a politically sensitive issue in a pre-election period, for example, could simply cause an entrenchment in their position, making a reversal of policy at a later stage more difficult.

## 6.5 Communicating with your audiences

Once you have analysed your audiences and decided on a mix of actions you will need to adapt the campaign messages to fit the appropriate audience sophistication level and the medium.

**Tips for creating successful messages**

**Keep the messages simple**
(even if the content is complex) – a 60 page report will still need an easily digestible summary. The campaign demands need to be communicated in clear, unambiguous language. One complaint heard continuously from policy makers is that VCOs are not clear enough about the precise action they want. What exactly do you want? Spell it out.

**Ensure your message has internal buy-in**
go back to when you framed your issue. Has this changed for any reason? It is imperative that all parts of the organisation adhere to the same message and campaign demands. This is equally applicable to partners in networks, coalitions and alliances.

**Keep repeating the same message over and over (and over!)**
you are competing with hundreds of others for the ear of decision makers and you need consistency and persistence to penetrate. You can say the same message repeatedly using many different formats and media.

## The right mix of persistence and opportunism

Political and social change takes time. And the message from past campaigns is that you should never be scared of sounding like a scratched record. Repetition is key. Your campaign message may be getting boring for you but it won't be for others. You will need to be persistent to win. This means finding innovative ways to keep pumping out the same message, seizing on opportunities as they arise and creating new ones, but in most cases always looking to repeat the same core message.

This was the approach adopted by the Labour Party before the 1997 general election. They had five key simple pledges that were played and replayed over and over on TV and radio, in leaflets, through megaphones, on postcards, pledge cards, street stalls, mugs, balloons, badges, speeches, banners, on giant street posters. Yet even on election day, some of the messages had not permeated the public awareness. You cannot say it often enough.

When compiling your materials bear in mind the AIDA formula:

| A | Attract **attention** | People are flooded with information. Unless your message can attract attention in the first place, it will have no opportunity to do anything. |
|---|---|---|
| I | Generate **interest** | Your audience has to be able to relate to and be interested in your message or the issue. |
| D | Encourage a **desire** to respond | People may be aware of a statistic or set of circumstances but lack the moral and emotional conviction to do anything about it. Your communication has to persuade them to want to do something by convincing them that what you say is true and important. Highlight the benefits of your approach – to them and to others. |
| A | Prompt **action** | Recommend specific action and make sure it is something the audience feels empowered and able to do. |

Campaigners today need to be as imaginative as possible to attract attention. It is a crowded world where are all bombarded by a maelstrom of messages through a myriad of media – to break through this noise you need to find a novel way of attracting attention. Find things that grab the attention and be creative – find ways of adapting them so that they can carry your message to your target.

- Shape (a campaign about youth justice) sent all MPs and journalists a 'police evidence bag' which contained 'evidence' that could be used in articles and debates.
- The BBC sent all MPs a video of the final episode of Morse in support of their campaign on TV licensing, knowing that they would probably be voting when it was broadcast.
- Fair Trade coffee tastings for council officials and councillors persuaded them to use it.
- Setting up mock minefields on beaches and in town centres drew public and media attention to the random effect of landmines.

Orchestrating a campaign mix of different tactics can seem like juggling with eels. It is useful to organise the activities into a system. A communications grid may be useful tool here:

| audience = route to influence key target (Health Minister) | campaign action | materials/ resources required | timescale | delegated to |
|---|---|---|---|---|
| Health Select Committee members (MPs) | written evidence to HIV hearing | case studies; FAQ sheet; briefing meeting | June 2005 | policy officer |
| Royal College of Nursing | action mailing; RCN Management Committee meeting; National HIV conference | direct mail pack; HIV speaker; video film; stall materials (posters, leaflets, branded items, TV and video) | Sept 2005 | campaign team lead and press office support |

Obviously this is a simplistic example. The grid can include type of message, phases of activity (for example direct mail followed by telephone call, followed by fulfilment device when replies received etc.). The important thing is that all activities are set out in a common framework that is shared between the key internal stakeholders and that has been focused through using the campaign cycle. This serves several purposes: it avoids duplication of approaches to influencers; it promotes accountability from staff; and it facilitates monitoring of outputs and subsequent redirection of activities if necessary. The campaign grid becomes a working and ever evolving document that is owned by all the relevant players in the organisation from the media/press office to policy staff, the campaign team and even fundraisers.

One other aspect of communicating the message that is sometimes underplayed is who is going to deliver it. People are more likely to respond positively to a message if they trust its source. This level of trust depends on your own organisational credibility as well as the 'attractiveness' of the person with the public face. In many cases, it is better to get impartial endorsement from an unexpected quarter; your own arguments can be dismissed with 'well they would say that, wouldn't they'. Instead of gathering only natural allies around you, think too about who is most likely to give their support to your cause and then seek to get them to back your campaign.

The best communication practice is built on telling personal stories – the media in particular are more interested in voices of experience. The downside of this is that the message can

**People are more likely to respond positively to a message if they trust its source.**

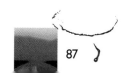

be uncontrollable. There are also practical difficulties where members of client groups cannot be used due to legal restraints or may prove unwilling, as they may (understandably) not want their photos taken.

## Learning points

You may wish to consider the following:

✓ The key principle in campaign delivery is to orchestrate a combination of campaign tactics to hit home the message to the key target in powerful and compelling ways.
✓ Do you understand your audience? Ask key questions about how they access information; what they read, see and hear.
✓ Have you identified your campaign mix?
✓ Think about segmenting your supporters as you would your audiences.
✓ When developing your campaign actions – always question what your outcome will be.
✓ Is your message credible and are practical solutions available?
✓ Do your campaign messages fit the audience and the medium?
✓ Have you organised activities into a communications grid – identifying audience, action resources/materials, timescales and the person responsible?
✓ Think about adapting the grid to your needs.

1. Grant, W (2000) Pressure Groups and British Politics. Macmillan Press Ltd
2. Cohen, D, de la Vega, R and Watson, G (2001) *Advocacy for Social Justice: A Global Action and Reflection Guide*. Kumarian Press Inc.
3. adapted from an original idea by John Barraclough, ex-campaigns writer, Oxfam
4. adapted from Keck, M and Sikkink, K (1998) *Activists Beyond Borders: Advocacy Networks in International Politics*. Cornell University Press
5. Adapted from membership trapezoid in Iliffe, S (2004) *The Good Membership Guide for the Voluntary Sector*. NCVO
6. Jordan, G and Maloney, W (1997) *The Protest Business? Mobilizing Campaign Groups*. Manchester University Press
7. Grant, W (2000) *Pressure Groups and British Politics*. Macmillan Press
8. Keck, M and Sikkink, K (1998) *Activists Beyond Borders: Advocacy Networks in International Politics*. Cornell University Press
9. Alinsky, S D (1989) *Rules for Radicals: A Pragmatic Primer for Realistic Radicals*. Vintage Books: Random House

# 7 Evaluation

"Give a woman a fish and feed her for a day, teach a woman to fish and feed her for a lifetime. Involve her in a campaign to maintain fish stocks, which is monitored and evaluated to ensure learning is shared and exploitation controlled, and enable future generations to feed themselves."
**adaptation of modern proverb**

It has already been argued that a monitoring and evaluation framework should be established at the planning stage. Evaluation is not something simply for bolting on at the end (see Section 5).

As part of this framework, it makes sense to establish an overall monitoring and evaluation timetable.

Monitoring, as has already been said, is ongoing throughout the duration of the campaign: evaluation occurs at periodic times within the lifetime of the campaign (and beyond, see point 5 below).

The figure on page 91 presents a notional approach to timetabling evaluation, although obviously the actual approach adopted will depend on the specific information needs of the particular campaign.

## Notes

1. It may make sense to consolidate campaign findings annually, although annual reviews of campaigning are more likely to fulfil organisational needs rather than the needs of the campaign (for which such rigid timetabling might prove somewhat artificial).

2. Where campaigns have a lifetime of more than a year, it may make sense to take the time to conduct a mid-term review, where progress so far can be assessed and lessons can be assimilated.

3. In some cases, if further funding is required, funders' reports may be needed prior to the campaign's completion (so that funding can be secured before the campaign ends) and this can be used as an opportunity to carry out a mid-term review or as preparatory work for a final evaluation.

4. A completion report is a tool for (a) looking back and making judgements about progress against objectives and (b) looking forward, and learning the lessons for future campaigning.

5. Given that much campaigning is long-term, campaigners should think about follow up reviews – so called ex-post evaluations [see timetable, page 91] – occurring after a campaign has finished. Distance of time often provides a more balanced context in which to consider the effects of the campaign. To take one example, the target of the campaign may no longer occupy the same position as they did at the time of the campaign and may therefore be more open to being honest about the influence of the campaign. There may also be unexpected results that do not become obvious until later.

## Learning point

You may wish to consider the following:

✓ Think about evaluation at the beginning of the campaign, not just at the end.

## Framework evaluation timeline for a notional 4-year campaign

| prior to launch | year one | year two | year three | year four | year five | year six |
|---|---|---|---|---|---|---|
| establish M & E framework and conduct baseline research | | | | | | |

monitor reports (e.g. quarterly or six monthly)

annual reviews

mid term review

update report for funders

completion report

ex-post evaluation

# Part three: Everything summarised

---

**...in which we set out a useful (and short) summary that the reader can use to access relevant information when most needed.**

# 8    Headlines

## 8.1 Effective campaigns

### 1. Campaign outputs need to effect outcomes to have an impact

The impact chain is a useful tool in understanding effective campaigning:

All campaigning involves making choices about the best way to achieve impact. Thinking through the stages of the impact chain helps make explicit your campaign choices – and the assumptions behind them. This should mean that your choices are better directed towards impact. To create an impact at the end of the chain you need to make the right choices at the beginning of the chain. Effort is important but it must be focused to be effective.

## 2. Managing a campaign based on the idea of a campaign cycle can help direct limited resources towards greatest impact

Expert campaign design is crucial for using limited resources most effectively. The campaigning cycle can be used as a guide through the stages of a campaign:

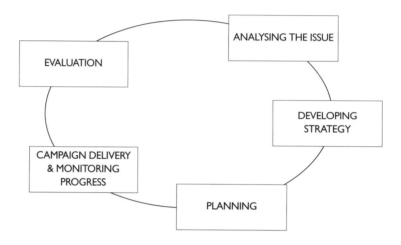

The cycle that we describe in Part One involves these five stages:
1. Analysing the issue and the context
2. Developing the campaign strategy
3. Setting objectives
4. Delivering and monitoring the campaign
5. Evaluating the campaign

## 3. Effective campaigns are based on a good understanding of the context in which they function

Analysing the issue and the context:
Time spent on analysing the problem, its causes and consequences, and on investigating possible solutions provides valuable information for your campaign. Analysis of the context – both external and internal – can also help in shaping the direction of the campaign.

**4. Developing a strategy – defining your broad approach towards your campaign aim – enables you to focus on how to achieve maximum impact for minimum investment**

Developing the campaign strategy:
You need a campaign aim that identifies the target of the campaign, the individual or group who needs to change for your desired change to happen. Identifying the routes of influence involves asking how much influence you (and your allies) have over the target, detecting where power lies, and identifying the best ways to have influence over the target (both directly and indirectly).

**5. Planning is important in ensuring that those working on the campaign are, together, delivering a coherent approach**

Setting objectives:
In many circumstances, it makes sense to plan in some detail. A written plan represents a way of helping internal audiences be clear about what is the campaign aim, what are the campaign objectives and what is happening, and when, to achieve them. A monitoring and evaluation framework should also be set up during the planning phase so that information can be gathered to assess – and learn from – the campaign's progress.

**6. The key principle in campaign delivery is to orchestrate a combination of campaign tactics to hit home the message to the key target in powerful and compelling ways**

Delivering and monitoring the campaign:
Choices of action will depend on all kinds of variables. The best campaigns are adapted to their particular circumstances, based on an understanding of key audiences and the best ways of influencing them.

**7. Evaluation should be thought about at the beginning of the campaign, not just at the end**

Evaluating the campaign:
This is a crucial component that is too often ignored or conveniently forgotten.

## Campaign checklist

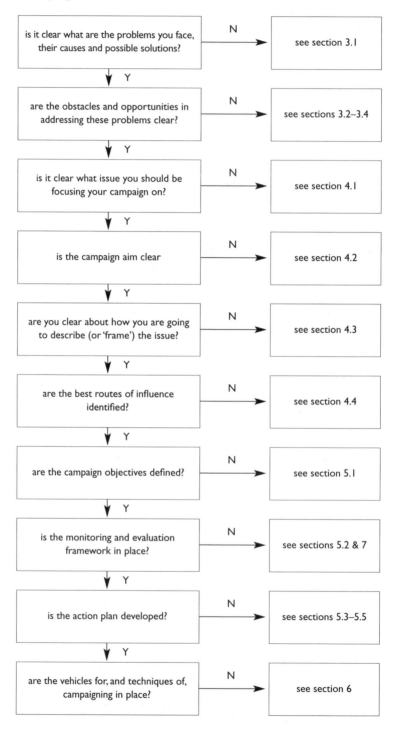

## 8.2 Effective campaigning organisations

An understanding of the campaign cycle helps with the examination of some of the issues in designing, developing, planning, delivering, monitoring and evaluating specific issue campaigns.

It may also be necessary for campaigners to explore some of the issues facing organisations that seek to deliver effective campaigning programmes. In other words, to examine the framework within which effective campaigning can flourish.

**8. Effective campaigning organisations understand how they function, where they stand and why they are doing what they are doing**

It is important for organisations that campaign to have clarity of purpose and to match aspirations to resources. Ensuring that an organisation is well-suited to the dynamics of campaigning requires clear campaign positioning and an understanding of the extent to which structures and cultures facilitate an effective campaigning programme.

**9. Collaboration with other organisations will almost always strengthen your campaign but all participants need to have a common understanding about the purpose and parameters of joint campaign activity**

Campaigning in collaboration with other organisations introduces new difficulties, but collaboration usually increases the likelihood of impact. If policy makers come to see that your partnership represents the views of the important players in your specific field of operation your campaign is more likely to make progress.

For partnership to be effective, it is important to have a common vision of how the collaboration will work and a common and openly stated understanding of how the campaign, and those engaged in it, will benefit from the collaboration.

**10. Monitoring and evaluating your campaign will help ensure that current campaigning activity is well-directed and that lessons are learned for future campaigning. Remember to plan for it and do it**

Monitoring and evaluation is just as important in campaigning as in other fields of operation, like service provision or fundraising. It is an easy part of the cycle to neglect or avoid, but the notion that it should not be attempted because it is too difficult is a mistaken one. Your campaigning will have more impact if you devote the appropriate resources, in the appropriate ways, to learning how to do it better.

## 11. Effective campaigning organisations understand the context in which they operate, and appreciate how they can achieve impact by gathering intelligence systematically

Developing a well-resourced campaign intelligence system will enable you to gather, and keep up to date, information that is relevant and necessary to guide effective campaigns and campaigning. You need to devote resources to building your own campaign intelligence system in your own way rather than relying on information sources that will not necessarily be tailored to your own needs.

## 12. Developing a deepening understanding of how change happens – and how your organisation can effectively intervene in the process of change – will ensure your campaign has greater impact

Campaigning is about effecting change. It therefore makes sense that the best campaigns are based on a robust understanding of change and why it happens – campaigns, campaigners and campaigning organisations will benefit from developing an appropriate theory of change.

## Campaigning checklist

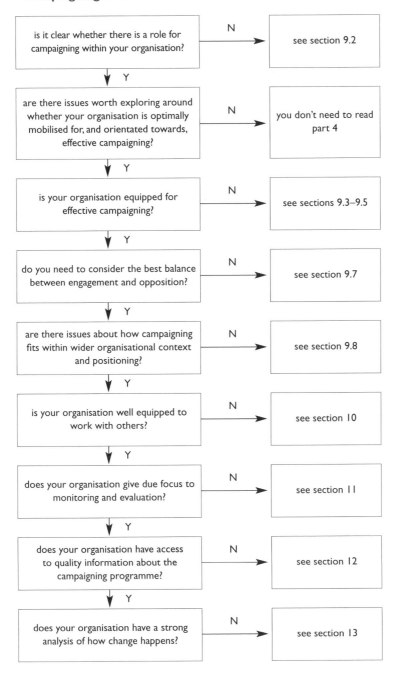

is it clear whether there is a role for campaigning within your organisation? — N → see section 9.2

Y

are there issues worth exploring around whether your organisation is optimally mobilised for, and orientated towards, effective campaigning? — N → you don't need to read part 4

Y

is your organisation equipped for effective campaigning? — N → see sections 9.3–9.5

Y

do you need to consider the best balance between engagement and opposition? — N → see section 9.7

Y

are there issues about how campaigning fits within wider organisational context and positioning? — N → see section 9.8

Y

is your organisation well equipped to work with others? — N → see section 10

Y

does your organisation give due focus to monitoring and evaluation? — N → see section 11

Y

does your organisation have access to quality information about the campaigning programme? — N → see section 12

Y

does your organisation have a strong analysis of how change happens? — N → see section 13

## 8.3 Summary of the summary

The best campaigners combine:
- a strong sense of strategy and planning – derived from a sophisticated assessment of the social and political environment in which they are operating and a realistic view of internal capacity and constraints
- a deep-rooted awareness of context – the ability to identify and exploit opportunity as it arises, based on an understanding of how change happens
- above all passion – the belief in and commitment to what they are doing and the tenacity and creativity to keep on doing it

This can be summed up in the following model:

One of these aspects on its own is unlikely to be enough. Campaigns can be made to work where two of these three qualities come together. But the heart of effective campaigning is the point at which all three converge.

The rest of this guide now looks at campaigning in more detail.

# Part four:
# The effective
# campaigning
# organisation

**... in which ways that your organisation could improve its approaches to campaigning are examined.**

# 9 Aspects of organisation

*"Change comes from power, and power comes from organisation."*
**Saul Alinsky, *Rules for Radicals***

## 9.1 Internal analysis

It is important to take into account the reality of your organisation's internal situation and match it to the aspirations you have to achieve impact with your campaigns.

In Part Two, some of the questions about internal capacity and constraints that it may be fruitful to ask in relation to the development of a specific campaign were identified. This section looks at ways in which you might consider how equipped your organisation is to be campaigning for impact.

Addressing the following questions may help with this process.

| Area | Key questions | See also ... |
|---|---|---|
| 1. clarity of purpose | • is the organisation's vision and mission clear?<br>• is it clear how campaigning fits within the organisation's mission and mandate? | Section 9.2 |
| 2. planning | • are the organisation's analysis and planning capabilities and resources adequate for its needs?<br>• are robust monitoring and evaluation systems in place? | Sections 2–7 on designing, developing and planning a campaign |
| 3. material resources | • does the organisation have sufficient funds, equipment and other resources?<br>• does it use resources efficiently? | Section 9.3 |
| 4. skills and expertise | does the organisation:<br>• have an understanding of political systems and the role of public opinion in campaigning?<br>• have access to quality policy information?<br>• have knowledge and use of multiple campaigning strategies?<br>• have staff with skills and competencies for campaigning?<br>• seek outside help when it needs it? | |
| 5. legitimacy, credibility and accountability | • does the organisation speak with legitimacy?<br>• are its messages trusted?<br>• are the staff, board and managers accountable to beneficiaries? | Section 9.4 |
| 6. orientation | • does the structure of the organisation facilitate its campaigning work?<br>• are you in a position to work collaboratively with others?<br>• are decision-making mechanisms clear and transparent?<br>• do campaign leaders have the support of board, staff and members? | Sections 9.5–9.7 |

## 9.2 Clarity of purpose

There is a trend towards more and more VCOs adopting campaigning as part of their range of activities. This growth is most likely being driven by a mix of internal factors (a recognition based on programme experience of the need to address root causes, for example) and external factors (in response to donor trends, for example).

Every decision to do one thing rather than another has an opportunity cost. And with resources limited, there needs to be a good case for why they should be dedicated to campaigning.

Allocating resources to campaigning as opposed to (or more likely in addition to) programming may make sense, for example, if you can show that by campaigning you can successfully resolve an issue that you otherwise have to raise funds to deal with at a more local level. For instance, your organisation may currently fund a service that you feel should be better provided by a local authority. If you run a campaign that successfully argues for the local authority to provide the service, this could be a more effective use of resources, and of greater benefit to those whom you are trying to help, than dedicating effort to further fundraising yourself in order to ensure the service is provided.

Deciding whether to campaign is a key strategic question that should ultimately be underpinned by a judgement of the relative impact of different possible balances between campaigning and service delivery. The more evidence available to inform decisions about allocating resources to different organisational functions, the more that strategic decisions about funding and resourcing can be made on something more than guesswork. Questions to consider in making that judgement include the following:[1]

> **Deciding whether to campaign is a key strategic question that should ultimately be underpinned by a judgement of the relative impact of different possible balances between campaigning and service delivery.**

| Is campaigning a **suitable** option? | • does it fit with your organisational vision, mandate, positioning and priorities?<br>• given the problems you are tackling and the solutions you have identified, are you confident that campaigning will help you make the best use of your resources?<br>• does the development of a campaigning programme fit with the political and social environment in which you are operating? |
|---|---|
| Is campaigning a **feasible** option? | • is developing effective campaigns achievable, given the resources, skills, etc. you have available?<br>• have you assessed the potential risks and are they manageable? |
| Is campaigning an **acceptable** option? | • would campaigning fulfil, or ignore, the expectations of the people you work with, and others with an interest in what you do?<br>• how will current donors and other supporters react?<br>• is the notion of your campaigning supported by beneficiaries? |

## The Children's Society

To take just one example, The Children's Society set up in summer 2004 a new, dedicated campaigning function. The decision to establish a campaigns department came in this case as a result of a (financially-driven) review of vision, mission and strategy, as part of which the organisation looked hard at itself and its purpose.

It allowed The Children's Society to look beyond service provision and to collate views of children it works with, create policy positions based on their experiences and to use them as a basis for campaigning to challenge the conditions that damage children's lives. In the words of The Children's Society: "it's not enough to help a single child. We want to change the world."

The decision to take the organisation's campaigning agenda forward in a more structured way was felt both to build effectively on the programme experience and to respond better to the needs of the children the organisation supports.

There was also felt to be an opportunity, through campaigning, more clearly to articulate the values of the organisation. The Children's Society is thus moving its campaigning agenda forward on the basis of a 'one business' model in which the solutions-focused style of the campaigns support and enhance the broader organisational positioning, through, for example, carrying fundraising messages and helping to engage and energise supporters.

The decision to expand the campaigning programme was taken after examining not only the potential benefits but also the risks. On one hand, it is recognised, too aggressive campaigning could have the effect of damaging relations with key institutions, such as local authorities, that The Children's Society works with in its programme work (and some of whom are potential or actual funders); on the other, a too-cautious approach risks having only limited success, creating the prospect of cooption and compromising on its mission to serve children. Like other organisations, The Children's Society will be steering a narrow path between these twin campaigning perils.

Ensuring – and demonstrating – progress through campaigning will be a vital element of the programme and early attention is therefore being paid to establishing a robust framework for campaigning monitoring and evaluation.

Campaigning and service delivery can be mutually beneficial disciplines: experience on the ground providing the basis for a twin-track approach to change where direct benefit is delivered through programmes and projects; and the lessons from local-level experience is translated to wider arenas. Where this works well, it might be said to be the ultimate in successful voluntary sector programming.

**Twin-track approach to achieving social change**

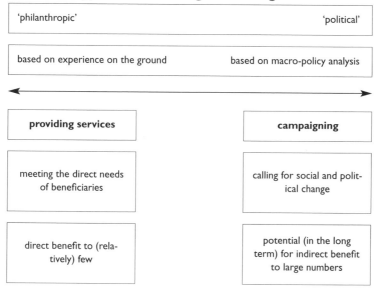

## 9.3 Resources

The resourcing of your campaigning function is obviously vital; in particular, it is important that you match your aspirations and ways of working to the resources available.

## Campaigning with limited resources[2]

|  | where your organisation has it | where your organisation lacks it |
| --- | --- | --- |
| money | • invest in the campaign – materials, research, staff, etc.<br>• make sure you are accountable for resource use through robust monitoring and evaluation | • select an issue whose prospect of resolution fits with the resources you have available (e.g. one that can be resolved through discrete insider lobbying)<br>• if more public campaigning is required, focus on low input, high visibility activities (e.g. publicity stunts)<br>• consider whether there are any opportunities for securing campaign funding |
| policy research expertise | • conduct and publish your own research<br>• develop an expert profile through publications, conferences, etc. | • develop policy through use of other sources<br>• brief yourself through other credible publications |
| capacity for marketing research | • market test your ideas before going forward<br>• track progress through longitudinal research – tracking surveys, etc. | • take your messages direct to your audiences and get feedback that way<br>• focus on low-cost ways of evaluating progress towards objectives |
| contacts | • maintain contacts systematically<br>• get introduced to successors when contacts move on<br>• deepen the network by introducing colleagues to contacts | • identify a set number of priority targets and try to meet them regularly<br>• try to maximise personal contact in ways that build trust |
| base of supporters | • mobilise supporter base to act as required throughout the campaign | • work with a core of active supporters if needed<br>• focus your effort (e.g. on target constituencies) |
| popular support | • use the media to ensure that your message is regularly heard | • consider using the media to try and create and amplify a sense of interest in the issue |

| skills to plan and deliver multiple campaign strategies | • maximise opportunity through using different strategies, operating in different arenas<br>• work with others who provide added campaign value | • identify the niche your organisation fulfils and seek to work with groups that complement your contribution |
| --- | --- | --- |

## Big or Small?

We asked for a view from the frontline about how campaigning differs in big and small organisations and received the following contribution from Jonathan Ellis of the Empty Homes Agency:

"My first experience of running a national campaign was with a large development charity. As a campaign manager, I relished developing a campaign with the benefit of using a household name; this also helped massively with establishing partnerships with other organisations, including those outside the sector – people wanted to work with us. I was also able to tap into the available resources to fund all of the materials for the campaign. Another huge benefit was knowing that the campaign would first be promoted to the thousands of campaign supporters that would help give the campaign a great start. Although getting sign-off on campaign materials was an arduous process due to the size of the organisation and the number of fingers in the pie, once you had sign-off you knew there was no going back.

Yet it was not a bed of roses. The sign-off procedure was painful and could take ages. And as a result, it was very difficult to be agile and respond to events. There was also the problem of conflicting priorities. I was running only one of three global campaigns, which was tricky enough. But there were also the priorities of the programme, fundraising, media and trading parts of the organisation. Campaigning was just one small part of the organisation and my campaign was an even smaller part of that.

After this experience, despite a successful outcome to the campaign, I resolved to work for a much smaller charity. At the Empty Homes Agency with just eight members of staff, we focus on just one issue. We can also respond with amazing speed to opportunities to promote the campaign. From the start, there was an exhilarating sense of freedom. I also noticed that it was so much easier to work with other organisations. Being so small we were much less precious about our brand and indeed to be seen to be working with larger groups only enhanced our brand.

Yet here again it was not ideal. In making the change I went from being a Campaign Manager to a Chief Executive – yes I could enjoy all the benefits above but I also had to run the charity. In addition, whilst I was passionate about my new organisation, I realised that few people had heard of us – I'd lost name recognition. Resources to run the campaign were also a challenge. Funders will fund projects, but how can small charities fund campaigns? We also lacked any membership base or media and policy departments.

The one thing that I have learned is that there is no ideal answer to the question posed: big is not necessarily best and small is not necessarily perfectly formed. You can get results in both big and small organisations. The ideal is to maximise the benefits depending upon where you find yourself. In my case at the moment, I am relishing the freedom of working for a small charity but trying to back up our campaigning by partnership work with bigger names such as Shelter and the TGWU. And our campaign has resulted in new empty homes powers being included in the Housing Act. In campaigning size isn't the issue – it is passion and focus!"

## 9.4 Legitimacy, credibility, accountability

**It is important that you can demonstrate your right to speak on an issue and for your voice to be trusted and respected.**

Legitimacy, credibility and accountability are vital to your ability to influence others.[3] These notions go to the heart of your organisation's reputation, which is a vital component of success. It is important that you can demonstrate your right to speak on an issue and for your voice to be trusted and respected.

### 9.4.1 Legitimacy

Your organisation should have a clear sense of whom you are speaking for and with what authority.

If in your campaign you aim to speak on behalf of beneficiaries, how can you be sure that the goal you have defined addresses their needs? How can you demonstrate this to those who might call into question your right to speak for others?

## Sources of legitimacy

Legitimacy can come from a range of sources, for example:
- as a result of personal, direct, practical experience on the ground;
- from the promotion of a particular value that is widely recognised within society and/or enshrined in law (e.g. equality legislation);
- through the ability to act as an expert on a particular issue;
- from other members of a network to which you belong possessing one or more of the above.

If you cannot demonstrate legitimacy in your campaigning, the danger is that:
- your campaign will be less powerful – people who are campaigning from a basis of direct experience will be more passionate and more effective at calling for change;
- there could be a lack of relevant information feeding into the campaign, with the possible consequence that the campaign won't be able to detect or respond to changes on the ground;
- the lack of access to evidence may result in an inability to engage in detailed debate as the terms of discussion shift, for example towards looking at the specific details of resolution;
- your campaign may be susceptible to counter-attack (by offended targets for example) as unrepresentative, inaccurate or irrelevant.

It is important to be clear on what basis you claim legitimacy and you need to consider how to rebut any challenge that your opponents may make. This means in particular that, when legitimacy is claimed on the basis of representation:
- systems of accountability need to be in place (see below);
- you should have evidence of the strength of your membership/support and how many of your supporters will directly benefit from the impact of victory in your campaign.

When legitimacy is claimed on the basis of experience, the way that you present your research will need explicitly to demonstrate

**It is important to be clear on what basis you claim legitimacy.**

the extent of your organisation's direct experience of the issue. This will not only give your campaign enhanced legitimacy but also, if people are prepared (and in a position) to speak out from personal experience, they will convey messages with greater force and credibility.

### 9.4.2 Credibility

It is of the utmost importance that your statements and motives are credible and can be trusted.

**Credibility is the brand equity of your organisation.**

Credibility is the brand equity of your organisation. A campaign can stand or fall by the extent to which it is seen by public and institutional audiences to be supported by credible organisations known for providing reliable information that is seen as being both expert and trustworthy. The testimony of credible witnesses works in the field of campaigning as well as in a court of law. Trust and respect come from a track record of delivery built up over time. If you have a credible reputation, protect it, as it is hard to regain respect if a single, but catastrophic, error of judgement is made.

---

### Sources of credibility

- the quality of information you provide;
- Scale measures such as the size of your organisation, numbers of supporters, etc.;
- the status of your board members and high profile supporters;
- your personal relations and the extent of your contacts and links;
- your policy analysis and expert knowledge;
- your perceived independence and objectivity;
- the representative nature of your relationship with beneficiaries.

---

With credibility and legitimacy your campaign will have greater impact but it is also important that an organisation can demonstrate to whom it is accountable.

### 9.4.3 Accountability

Accountability can usefully be sub-divided into:
- functional accountability (to donors and the board, for example, for the way that you use resources); and
- strategic accountability (for the impact that your actions have on intended beneficiaries and others).

You owe it to yourself and to beneficiaries to maximise your accountability for achieving change through the campaigning programme. It is not an optional add-on; any VCO that has decided to undertake campaigning should examine how account-able it is to the people it seeks to support.

---

## Sources of accountability

- frequency of direct contact with beneficiaries;
- openness of decision making;
- the extent to which monitoring and evaluation is embedded in planning;
- willingness to be transparent in evaluation by communicating your progress to others outside the organisation;
- the power of the voice and visibility of partners and beneficiaries in the organisation.

---

## 9.5 Power and influence

Through campaigning, you are seeking to influence targets, within public audiences and/or within institutions. Power is that which enables you to have this influence.

Power is therefore a key concept in campaigning and it may be worth taking time to identify and deconstruct the different sources of power available to you, and the extent to which you have, or don't have, power in your engagement with different campaign audiences. The following table summarises some sources of power that may be of relevance to your organisation:[4]

## Levers of power

| power lever | in relation to public audiences | in relation to institutions |
|---|---|---|
| coercive | • not relevant, unless it could be construed that your organisation seeks to coerce people into supporting your campaign. | • you may have, for example, the ability to impede policy, or exert economic or legal leverage on the target;<br>• in addition, you may have the power (although you may not wish to use it) to attack and put pressure on a particular institution through direct action, such as a public demonstration. |
| reward | • by giving you their support, people associate themselves with your values;<br>• your success also brings benefits to supporters and/or members by giving expression to their own interests and values.[5] | • you may be in a position where you can 'reward' or 'punish' the target through public praise or criticism. |
| legitimate | The recognition that you have the right to speak on a particular issue can be because, for example:<br>• the issue impacts on your organisation's public work;<br>• your organisation has some form of statutory or official status within a particular policy arena; or<br>• it is clear that you represent others.<br>Perceived legitimacy gives you much greater authority to speak out. | |
| expert | • through its background and experience, your organisation will have built brand equity; this will be easier in some circumstances than in others (e.g. bigger organisations whose demands are in harmony with general cultural norms tend to command general respect).[6] | • in lobbying and direct engagement, you may well know more about the issue of concern than the official or minister you are talking to;<br>• your power can be built up over time by establishing a sense that your contributions to policy debate are reliable and of a consistently high quality. |
| personal and connection | All kinds of contacts and links bring you added ability to influence public and institutional audiences; but the caveat is that these relationships tend to be personal, not institutional. Where this is the case, there is a need for the organisation to:<br>• keep a good paper trail that others might follow;<br>• exploit opportunities for expanding others' contacts. | |
| information | You may have resources or information that audiences want; if so, this gives you increased bargaining power. | |

In thinking about power, it is worth also considering the following:[7]

- **power is dynamic** – it changes all the time;
- **power is relative** – it's not something you either have or don't have;
- **power is domain-specific** – you may have power in one arena but none in another;
- **power is perceived** – sources of power are dependent on the audience's perception of the organisation, rather than on any objective reality. Therefore an organisation's power will vary significantly between different audiences;
- **power is a balance of forces** – this is perhaps the most important thing and sometimes the easiest to forget. Your campaign is not happening in isolation; when thinking about your power and its sources, analyse your opponents' power too.
- **power is subjective** – so that, for example, it relies on factors such as the reasonableness of your demands, or your ability to talk the same language. Your acceptability and interest to government may also depend on its perception of the 'attractiveness' of the client group you represent in terms of both its potential electoral influence and how 'deserving' it is.

## Power and perception

Over the years, the Countryside Alliance deployed a number of arguments in favour of hunting, moving from disputing the allegation of cruelty, to the issue of jobs, the rights of minorities, etc.

One argument that seemed to be initially successful was their suggestion that the strength of feeling in the countryside was in favour of hunting. Largescale demonstrations appeared to bear this out and probably had the effect of making the Government more reluctant to support a fox-hunting ban. To counter this perception, the League Against Cruel Sports and its allies commissioned a poll of those on some of these marches and found, significantly, that 82 per cent of marchers with a political preference professed to be Conservative voters. Less than half were truly rural.

This, together with the fact that a number of anti-hunting Labour MPs in rural constituencies were targeted in 2001 by pro-hunt campaigners, with no discernible effect, was helpful in convincing Labour MPs who favoured a ban that there was less electoral risk in supporting a ban than the press were assuming.

## 9.6 Structure and culture[8]

### 9.6.1 Fit with the environment

Different types of organisation work better in different environments. To be most effective, the various aspects of an organisation (its structure, culture and management decision-making, for example) need to be both:

- internally consistent; and
- appropriate to the environment in which that organisation operates.

Organisations working for social change tend to work in environments that are politically uncertain and therefore turbulent rather than stable. In general, campaigning is a non-routine discipline.

The implications of this are that:

- campaigning organisations need to be strategically proactive, recognising that the context for campaigning is constantly changing, rather than assuming it stays the same;
- at the operational level, in campaign delivery the need is to maximise flexibility by being quick – expediting decisions about the progress of the campaign, for example – and being agile, exploiting opportunities as they arise.

This suggests the need for:

- good information flows that are both speedy and two-way;
- freedom and flexibility for campaigners to take decisions, to take risks and try out new things.

The evidence is that bureaucratic structures are not well equipped to deal with fast-changing environments. In such cases, the centre can become a bottleneck or in the worst cases a tourniquet.

It would seem that more complicated decision-making structures (for instance matrix management) introduce levels of complication best avoided in campaigning (if they can be). Effective campaign organisations tend to eschew bureaucracy for more dynamic and creative structures. This means delegating decision making to the front line, fostering leadership and innovation, and supporting risk-taking.

The case studies for this book bear out that even those campaigners who work within relatively bureaucratic organisations tend to be most successful by creating (or having created for them) a space where the bureaucracy doesn't reach.

**Effective campaign organisations tend to eschew bureaucracy for more dynamic and creative structures.**

---

### Hierarchical or democratic decision making?

Hierarchy can give speed and a clear sense of direction. But distance from the ground can mean that decision makers are ill-informed and decisions made with inadequate information. Democratic decision making can maximise the energy of the grassroots. Decentralised structures can however result in disjunction and lack of a coordinated effort. The danger is, too, that opportunities for participation may be little more than symbolic – decision making in some groups has been described as more like 'anticipatory oligarchy'[9] where decisions are made by a few in the belief that the many will support them.

Getting the balance right is a question of developing campaigns within a 'simultaneous loose-tight organisation'[10] where there is some tight central control of values and principles within which context many things have been delegated to the frontline. Arguments can be made for either hierarchical or delegated control, but not for structures where decision making is dissipated and lines unclear.

---

Whatever the structure, speed and agility are crucial factors in campaigning and yet so many delays can occur at different stages in campaign delivery, especially within bigger organisations.

## Assessing flexibility

One way to deal with this is through a flexibility audit, identifying and isolating the reasons for delay and then dealing with them:

- how quickly is information that you need for the continuing development of the campaign reaching you?
- how quickly can the people that need this information access and interpret it?
- how quickly can you change tactics and approaches if the situation warrants it?
- who needs to be involved in decision making? If it involves a group or a team, does this group meet regularly? Can it be convened quickly? Can ad hoc decisions be made by individuals as representatives of the wider group? What sensitivities might this create within the organisation or network? How can they be addressed?
- how quickly can changes be communicated to those responsible for implementation?
- how can you keep planning agile so that plans be kept relevant without too much valuable time being spent updating them?
- can you organise your techniques to have a quicker turnaround, e.g. through urgent action emails, phone trees?

### 9.6.2 Promoting learning

It seems to be the case that aspects of the culture of VCOs can often militate against campaign learning.[11]

This may manifest itself, for instance, in one or more of the following:

- a dominant activist culture in which action is valued and reflection seen as an unaffordable luxury, or even an unnecessary diversion;
- a prevailing sense that criticism, even self-criticism, detracts from a carefully cultivated image of success, which is needed for positioning, to raise funds etc.;
- under-resourcing, with the result that recording or sharing of learning is deprioritised – evaluations of campaigning in the VCO sector are still relatively rare;
- a desire for quantifiable results (from the board for example), which does not usually sit easily with the

most appropriate methodologies for evaluating campaigns (which tend to be more naturalistic and qualitative – see Section 11);

- a reluctance to take risks and therefore a reliance on a kind of campaigning template that may be outdated and in need of renewal;
- authority residing within a management team that is reluctant to delegate and yet meets insufficiently often to supply the agility needed for effective campaigning;
- an unwillingness to acknowledge and thus deal with tensions of values, purposes, strategy and tactics between different parts of the organisation – tensions that may as a result constrain campaigning (see Section 9.7);
- widespread trepidation towards the idea of evaluating campaigns, something regarded as being too difficult to embark on.

And yet campaigning without learning is like Oliver Hardy without Stan Laurel. Who remembers *The Fighting Kentuckian* (in which only one member of the duo appeared)?

Campaigning is not a routine discipline: it does not take place in stable environments; it takes place in turbulence, at the edge of chaos. A place, above others, where there is a need for what is termed double loop learning – taking a 'double look' at the situation by questioning the relevance of accepted ways of operating norms (see step 2a below).

**Double loop learning[12]**

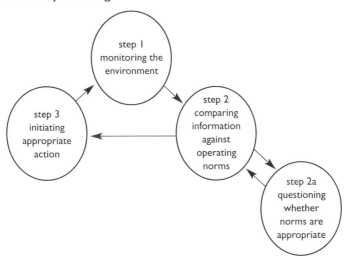

**Not only should campaign activities be adapted as the campaign develops but also that objectives themselves should invariably be changed or adapted to fit with changed circum-stances.**

This means, for example, that not only should campaign activities be adapted as the campaign develops – in order to improve achievement of a particular objective – but also that objectives themselves should invariably be changed or adapted to fit with changed circumstances.

The concept of double loop learning encourages this kind of approach by building in an extra step (2a) where assumptions are questioned, enhancing the prospects that the campaign will adapt and reorganise accordingly. Ways of promoting this kind of self-questioning include:

- designing accessible and evolving networked information systems to promote free flow of information;
- encouraging multi-skilled teams, not highly specialised jobs;
- creating maximum autonomy by minimising rules and restrictions – defining no more than is necessary.[13]

### 9.6.3 Orientation

The best campaigning organisations are concerned primarily with the external environment, not bogged down disproportionately by internal considerations. Two aspects of this are particularly important.

1. an interest/commitment/belief in the issue
2. a concern to understand and engage with target audiences

Where both of these factors are strongly held, our judgement and experience is that organisations tend to be effective at campaigning. Low interest in one or the other (or both) can have detrimental effects on the campaigning programme.

## Orientations in campaigning[14]

| | | Low | Medium | High |
|---|---|---|---|---|
| Degree of focus on the issue | High | **Unfocused campaigns:** messages do not reach, or do not resonate with, key audiences | | **Effective campaigns:** effort is coordinated and targeted at achieving change |
| | Medium | | **Unadventurous campaigns:** a standard template tends to be followed no matter what the context | |
| | Low | **Impoverished campaigns:** internal considerations dominate | | **Marketing-led campaigns:** branding may be a more important consideration than impact |
| | | Low | Medium | High |
| | | Degree of focus on target audiences | | |

## 9.7 Insider or outsider?

Are you on the inside track, working constructively with the target to reach a solution and/or are you a political outsider putting pressure on the target through challenge or conflict?

### A ban on fox-hunting?

As a result of the way that the Labour Government handled the fox-hunting debate between 1997 and 2004, expectations of both sides of the debate were raised that the issue could be resolved in their favour. Whilst the Government showed unmistakeable signs of unwillingness to progress the ban, no Minister said definitively that a ban would not be introduced. Given this, amidst hundreds of hours of Parliamentary time dedicated to the issue, numerous rounds of consultations, relentless searches for compromise, the mooting of different options, the Burns

Inquiry, etc., the League Against Cruel Sports consistently recognised the prospect of Government legislation as the only game in town. After the Foster Bill ran out of Parliamentary time, the evidence was clear that a ban would not be enacted through a Private Members Bill, in which case the campaign needed the Government on side to achieve its aim.

Therefore, throughout periods of delay and doubt, it was a question of the campaign holding its nerve, whilst taking steps in turn to maintain the resolve of MPs (many of whom championed the ban and who themselves had certain expectations of the Government) and to focus their concerns on getting the Government to enact legislation. Although there were times when optimism was low, it never reached the point where it made sense to accuse the Government of betraying its commitment to facilitate the banning of hunting – apart from anything else, such an approach risked giving permission to the Government to pursue just such a course.

With time running out in the 2003–04 Parliamentary Session for the Hunting Bill to be reintroduced (in order to invoke the Parliament Act), in the end it seemed to be the Countryside Alliance that increasingly resorted to outsider tactics, an approach that may have backfired, in that the vociferousness of their protest may have enhanced Government desire to see the issue finally cleared from the legislative agenda.

The typology of 'insider' and 'outsider' campaigning organisations provides one particularly useful way to think about your positioning.[15] The difference can be summarised as follows:

| | Insiders | Outsiders |
|---|---|---|
| orientation | concentrate on solutions | tend to focus on problems |
| approach | willing to engage in constructive dialogue | conflictual; reject the idea of 'co-option' |
| focus | lobbying, behind closed doors | public campaigning, e.g. through direct action |
| advantages | listened to and may have direct influence on policy | perceived by supporters to be active; 'untainted' by compromise |

| | | |
|---|---|---|
| disadvantages | danger is of regressing to 'prisoner' status: for example, a target's motivation for engagement may sometimes be a delaying tactic instead of representing a genuine desire jointly to develop sound policy recommendations | • opportunities for influence may be blocked: "Many decisions are clearly taken within relatively closed policy networks in which the complexity of the problems being discussed often constitutes a significant entry barrier"[16]<br>• may alienate target instead of influencing them positively |

As organisations grow and mature, the evidence is that they tend to shift towards insider status – partly for strategic reasons – based on the recognition that to avoid being excluded from participation they need to move into the inside track – but also because mature organisations tend to be less willing to take risks.

However, some choose to remain on the outside as that is how they want to be perceived – they wish to be seen as activist campaigning organisations that are challenging the powerful without compromising their integrity.

## The 4Cs of the inside track[17]

- consultation
- consent
- cooperation
- continuity in the policy making process

There is also a fifth C compromise: "... a key and beautiful word ... If you start with nothing, demand 100 per cent, then compromise for 30 per cent, you're 30 per cent ahead".[18]

## The virtue of compromise

As the Housing Bill progressed through Parliament, Citizens Advice was keen that legislation relating to tenants' deposits should be incorporated within it. In order to secure this, their analysis was that a deal could be made that incorporated some of the concerns of landlords' representative organisations (who argued that their own members were subject to self regulation and therefore should be able to continue to hold the deposit money themselves as long as this was backed by insurance).

The campaign assessment was that the benefits – in terms of securing the ultimate progress of the legislation – of getting the Association of Residential Letting Agents (ARLA) on board outweighed any cost, in terms of allowing for more than one type of tenancy deposit protection scheme. Indeed the Government pilot had tested both custodial and insurance backed options, both of which had proved to meet the needs of tenants and landlords The campaign therefore lobbied the Government – together with ARLA – that all deposits should be protected through being part of a government-approved scheme, which could be either custodial or insurance backed.

Given Citizens Advice's judgement that it was possibly the best chance in a generation to get progress on the issue, it made sense to compromise and thus build a wider coalition of support for change, especially given the evidence that the major problems for tenants were indeed caused by those landlords who operated outside any existing self-regulatory framework.

**The distinction between insider and outsider approaches could be said to reflect the distinction between lobbying and public campaigning.**

To some extent, the distinction between insider and outsider approaches could be said to reflect the distinction between lobbying and public campaigning.

This interpretation is emphasised by the following model identifying the different approaches you could take in seeking to influence your target:[19]

| approach | technique | aim | outsider |
|---|---|---|---|
| attack | public campaigning | to weaken or eliminate the target organisation | |
| confront | | to force a change on the target organisation | |
| persuade | lobbying | to convince potential allies within the organisation through constructive argument | |
| cooperate | | to enter a process of joint learning by working with the organisation | insider |

These approaches undertaken by the same organisation may complement or conflict with each other.

You may find it difficult to use two different approaches (such as engagement through advocacy and public criticism) at the same time but if you can position yourself in this way, it enables you to get the best of both worlds.

### Confrontation or collaboration[20]

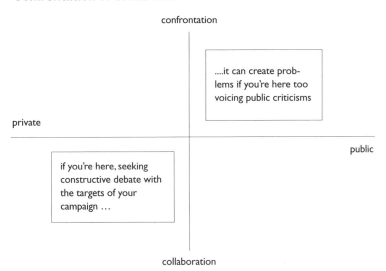

confrontation

....it can create problems if you're here too voicing public criticisms

private

public

if you're here, seeking constructive debate with the targets of your campaign ...

collaboration

---

### insider-outsider balance

One key early aspiration that The Salvation Army had for influencing the Gambling Bill during its initial (pre-legislative) stages was to establish itself as part of the policy debate. Following significant prepraration, the organisation gave evidence in front of a Parliamentary joint committee of MPs and Peers, and its performance and position seems to have been sufficiently impressive for The Salvation Army to be subsequently recognised, along with The Methodist Church, as the critical voice within the debate with whom the Government was prepared to liaise. This role was cemented over the following months, through regular contact with senior officials.

The Salvation Army considered the insider route to be important to maintain because of the advantages it brought, including access to information that would otherwise be unavailable and enhanced credibility with others outside government (such as the media). The judgement was based on the assessment that getting the Government to accept amendments was the most likely route to successful influence.

During the course of the Bill's development, the Government made concessions that The Salvation Army welcomed (for example over removing fruit machines from unlicenced premises) but concerns remained about the proposed expansion of casinos. Once the Bill was published, it very quickly became a high profile media story, which had its advantages in terms of exerting influence on the Government, but this snowballing of the campaign also had the effect of straining relations between The Salvation Army and ministers and officials. The press not being interested in nuanced criticism, it became very difficult to tread the line between responding to the media and maintaining the relationship with the Government. Overall the judgement was that relations were maintained during this difficult period, although not without hiccups. Factors that help to explain how it was done include that:

- there was recognition within Government of the legitimacy of The Salvation Army's campaign, based as it was on programme experience and a long track record of concern;
- in the early stages of the campaign, political capital had been built up and good personal relations established;
- much time was invested in direct contact with officials, and effort was made, for example, to explain the appearance of contentious coverage;
- every effort was made to distinguish between conversations on and off the record;
- the campaign never made personalised attacks, never criticised the Minister personally for example;
- efforts were made to acknowledge government concessions publicly.

Another way of operating a twin-track insider-outsider strategy is to develop an understanding with another organisation and decide to adopt different positions. An outsider organisation can then drive your target into the arms of an insider organisation. The outsiders make the noise and convince people that there is a problem: the insiders help resolve this problem for the policy makers. Everyone is happy.

---

### War on Want

War on Want – an overseas development agency has – traditionally developed campaigns on topics that other organisations feel are too controversial to pursue. It is proud of this role and is respected for it by other organisations.

It first campaigned on trade and debt in the 1950s. It called for the terms of trade and loan provisions to be altered to allow developing countries fair access to markets and finance in the developed world. In the 1970s, it launched a shareholder action campaign against tea companies and a campaign against the promotion of baby milk substitutes. In the 1980s, it developed a popular campaign on debt and the role of women in development. In the 1990s, it campaigned on the need to protect workers' rights in a globalised economy. It recently helped set up the Tobin Tax campaign to call for an international tax on currency speculation to provide resources for international development. These are all campaigns that have subsequently been taken up by others. Other organisations can leave War on Want to take up issues and to test public and policy-maker reaction in the secure knowledge that they will be clearing the way for others to follow.

War on Want is currently campaigning against the privatisation of public water companies in developing countries – arguing that the provision of international aid should not be conditional on the recipient government's adoption of a policy of privatisation of state utilities.

---

## 9.8 Organisational coherence

Many organisations that start as service providers gradually get more engaged in research and policy discussion, often leading to development of a campaigning programme. It is very rare for this process to be reversed.

### Mapping a trend towards campaigning

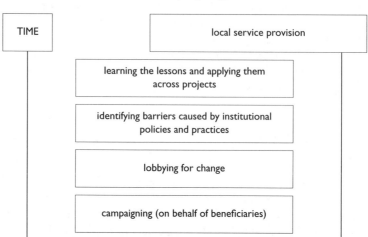

Perhaps because of this evolutionary process, sometimes, but not always, the campaigns function can be perceived by some as the cuckoo in the nest.

Our experience as practitioners and as evaluators is that in bigger organisations in particular there may be tensions between the campaigning, service provision, research and policy, communications and fundraising functions. There can be conflict over resources and – more fundamentally – disagreements over strategy and tactics can go to the heart of why the organisation exists and how it is trying to achieve its vision. In smaller organisations, when all of these functions are vested in fewer people, there is less potential for conflict within the staff but tensions can still arise, at board level for example.

Different organisations deal with conflict in different ways. It is probably true to say that in the VCS overt conflict tends to be avoided – but this doesn't mean it doesn't exist. There are a few words about some of the potential dimensions of conflict here because this is a potential problem that should not be ignored. In most cases, it is more appropriate to address this conflict and seek to use it to strengthen resolve and coherence, rather than hope it will go away.

### 9.8.1 Campaigning and service delivery

It has already been noted (see Section 9.2) how campaigning and service delivery can be mutually beneficial disciplines. There can, however, be tensions in how the two dovetail; for example:

- questions about the balance of resourcing may arise, pivoting on fundamental (and sometimes unresolved) questions about organisational mission and routes to impact;
- the two programmes might have different communication needs so that, for example, service users or beneficiaries may not be happy with campaign imagery and materials and the way that problems and issues are communicated through the campaign;
- issues about who speaks for whom may come to the fore;
- the dual approach can raise questions about the balance between partnership and targeting – through your campaign you might end up criticising the organisations who are (through your programming) funding your work.

The most effective way of neutralising these tensions is to give your beneficiaries a central role in developing and delivering the campaign. This helps root the campaign in the programme experience and gives the campaign added power through enhanced legitimacy, credibility and accountability.

### 9.8.2 Campaigning and policy research

Probably the most common disjunction is the one between campaigners and policy researchers.

Amongst the risks for campaigns are that the research produced may:

- not be tied to clear political goals;
- prioritise perfect over credible solutions;
- tend to be a primarily intellectual pursuit valuing peer review over contribution to the campaign goals;
- dictate the campaign timetable, rather than feeding into it (e.g. when the campaign ends up being planned round a series of report launches);
- be 'presented' to campaigners in unusable ways, with unclear target audiences;
- resist simplification (so that the campaign message becomes too opaque and obtuse for public audiences);

- convince internal audiences but not really be directed at what would convince external ones;
- use case studies and personal stories in a fragmented, not strategic, way;
- arrive late.

Campaigners' need for simplified, even simplistic, messages can, in turn, represent a threat to policy researchers. And in particular, the need for 'heroes and villains' tends not to chime with the real-life situation that the researchers are keen to represent.

In terms of campaign strategy, as well, the two can be out of accord. Researchers and policy lobbyists tend to be insiders, working through cooperation and persuasion, whereas campaign methodologies focus more on attempting to force change through confrontation and even attack. These different approaches can operate in tandem, but it requires a degree of sophistication that, if you don't have, can leave you exposed.

The way to avoid these kinds of problems is to ensure that the two disciplines are fully integrated in campaign development, planning and implementation, and not to give one primacy over the other. The two disciplines fit together best when there is mutual respect for role and remit and a joint commitment to ensure that the power of the campaign is not diminished by conflict over control of resources and functions.

## The Cystic Fibrosis Trust

The Cystic Fibrosis Trust ran a long-term campaign to achieve a national screening programme for babies in order to detect the disease from birth. If diagnosed early and given appropriate treatment, the prognosis and quality of life for cystic fibrosis sufferers could be significantly improved. Unfortunately for the Trust, the scientific evidence could not prove a definite and unambiguous link between early screening and long-term patient improvement, despite the wealth of anecdotal and clinical evidence available to support this claim. This proved a major sticking point for the Government's scientific advisory committee and a barrier to achieving the campaign aim.

After assessing the situation The Cystic Fibrosis Trust, working through a female Labour MP, decided to redirect its campaign strategy. Recognising that the new Minister responsible for the issue was a woman and expecting a child at the time, the Trust chose to run an insider campaign to appeal to her good sense and instincts, combined with strong clinical evidence from experts in the disease. It amassed a wealth of personal testimonies from families of people with cystic fibrosis, pulled together a group of eminent physician specialists and sought out policy evidence from other countries that had adopted screening programmes, backed by independent research from several countries.

The evidence was presented direct to the Minister in an sdjournment debate in Parliament, at private meetings with the Minister and MPs and with the Trust. The quality and quantity of evidence, combined with a cooperative insider approach, eventually overcame the scientific opposition and the Government announced a national babies screening programme for cystic fibrosis in 2001.

### 9.8.3 Campaigners and fundraisers

Whilst there is some evidence that members' and supporters' campaigning activity tends to reinforce their donor action, there can still be tensions between campaigning and fundraising functions.

At a strategic level, these two functions tend to be underpinned by different values (about the core purpose of the organisation for example), a reality not always recognised or dealt with. Existing or potential donors may be put off by the representation of the organisation as a radical political campaigning organisation, for example, although in some cases this is of course the attraction. The fear of this type of 'donor fright' can also cause repercussions as it can militate against an agile campaign, if, for example there is increased caution about campaign messages, making sign-offs for materials and messages very laborious.

In organisations with supporters or members, too, questions about 'ownership of names' (for instance fundraisers want access the names of people recruited to the campaign and campaigners want access the names and addresses of people who are existing donors) may be difficult to resolve. And the timescales within which the two functions optimally operate are not naturally in harmony. Donor mailings are often meticulously planned months in advance, whereas campaigns work best when contact with supporters is opportunistic and reactive.

### 9.8.4 Campaigning and media work

Within VCOs, campaigners often have to work in close cooperation with press officers and other communication professionals.

This book does not seek to conflate campaigns and media
work – they are separate but mutually supportive functions. But,
as with colleagues in policy functions, there may be conflicting
purposes between campaigns and communications staff.

It may not be as obvious as with other functions, but a number
of campaigns have suffered from undue conflict. If the success of
media workers is measured in (both quantity and quality of)
coverage then there may well be a tendency to sacrifice the
campaign objective to seek publicity. If campaigners seek to be
too strident in their demands, some media will avoid covering
issues. It is usually a balancing act and, to ensure the balance is
kept, some organisational resources should be invested into speci-
fying how the two functions will work together.

Indeed this approach holds good for other functions discussed
– although it is important to avoid bureaucratic inertia, there
needs to be some mechanism to facilitate cross-organisational
working. This could be a steering group, a common workplan, or
ad-hoc meetings at key times. All three have been adopted and
they each have their own strengths and weaknesses.

---

### Effective cross-team working

Building on its own project experience, Barnardo's has
been campaigning on the sexual exploitation of children
since 1994. The approach has combined lobbying, media
pressure and multi-agency influencing as well as
preventative education in schools. One striking aspect of
Barnardo's campaigning is the way that a multi-
disciplinary team has stayed focused and maintained
agility in driving forward the campaign. Amongst the
factors that have promoted this are:

- the existence of a small core strategy group, with others
  brought in to advise and give support to the developing
  campaign as necessary;
- a common sense of purpose within the core team, with
  shared clarity about the long-term direction of the
  campaign;
- a willingness to agree on common positions despite any
  internal disagreements in reaching those positions;

- the proactive involvement of project staff in helping to shape the campaign so that the campaign ran in tandem with, and was an extension of, the programmes, tapping directly into on-the-ground experience;
- a recognition that effective campaigning involves synergy between different approaches (media advertising and policy lobbying, for example);
- a resistance to getting bogged down in detail, instead a widespread desire to keep pushing on;
- time invested in building and maintaining close working relations between members of the campaign team;
- senior members of the team being prepared to speak up for the campaign to the wider organisation;
- above all, a mutual respect for individuals' expertise and a strong joint commitment to the cause.

## Learning points

You may wish to consider the following:

✓ Effective campaigning organisations understand how they function, where they stand and why they are doing what they are doing.

✓ Have you carried out an internal analysis to establish internal capacity and constraints?

✓ Do your aspirations and ways of working match the resources available?

✓ Do you take time to identify and deconstruct the different sources of power available to you?

✓ Have you carried out a flexibility audit – identifying and isolating reasons for delay?

✓ Have you considered your organisation's status as an insider or outsider – and determined the balance between the two?

1. Johnson, G and Scholes, K (1989) *Exploring Corporate Strategy: Text & Cases*. Prentice Hall International (UK) Ltd
2. adapted from Campaign to Protect Rural England (2002) *Getting Organised & Getting Results*. CPRE at www.cpre.org.uk/publications/CPRE/campaigning.htm
3. sources and notions of power from Handy, C (1993) *Understanding Organizations* (4th Edition). Penguin Books and Kakabadse, A, Ludlow, R and Vinnecombe, S (1988) *Working in Organizations*. Penguin Books

4. see 3. above

5. Jordan, G and Maloney, W (1997) *The Protest Business? Mobilizing Campaign Groups*. Manchester University Press, pp82-83

6. as noted by Grant, W (2000) *Pressure Groups and British Politics*. Macmillan Press, pp207 and
Coxall, B (2001) *Pressure Groups in British Politics*. Pearson Education Ltd

7. from Handy, C (1993) *Understanding Organizations* (4th Edition). Penguin Books, Chapter 5

8. section 8.6 draws from organisational theory, in particular from Morgan, G (1998) *Images of Organization* (The Executive Edition), Berrett-Koehler Publishers Inc & Sage Publications Inc., Chapters 3, 4 & 8, and also
Peters, T (1998) *Thriving on Chaos: Handbook for a Management Revolution*. Macmillan London
Pugh, D and Hickson, D (1996) *Writers on Organization* (5th Edition). Penguin Books. Chapter on Tom Burns

# 10 Collaboration

*"The need of mutual aid and support which had lately taken refuge in the narrow circle of the family, or the slum neighbours, in the village, or the secret union of workers, re-asserts itself again, even in our modern society, and claims its rights to be, as it always has been, the chief leader towards further progress."*
**Peter Kropotkin, *Mutual Aid: A Factor of Evolution (1902)***

Given the enormity of the challenges faced by campaigners, most organisations see the sense in collaboration. While there is obviously strength in numbers, however, working with others can also present difficulties and frustrations.

This section looks at the types, benefits and challenges of collaborating with others in campaigning for impact.

## 10.1 The advantages and disadvantages of joint working

From the outset, it is important to be very clear what you want to achieve by working with others. This means identifying the anticipated benefits of collaboration. There will also be costs involved in forming, managing and maintaining the relationships and it makes sense to weigh up the cost/benefits of collaboration – both internally and externally with your potential partners – at an early stage. This is likely to be a helpful exercise to ensure that future problems are anticipated and attempts made to prevent them by building in coping strategies.

If you all start with common expectations and a common understanding of the rationale behind the decisions to collaborate you are less likely to encounter difficulties later on.

If you start with common expectations and a common understanding of the rationale behind the decisions to collaborate you are less likely to encounter difficulties later on.

Below are identified some of the most common benefits and challenges:

| Benefits of joint working | Potential pitfalls of joint working |
| --- | --- |
| • Ability to pool information sources and direct experience | • Members fiercely protect their own intelligence |
| • Increased access to decision makers – more influence routes opened | • Members protect their own contacts with decision makers |
| • Ability to reach and harness support of increased numbers of the public | • Members refuse access to supporter network |
| • Cross-organisational learning potential | • Power imbalances develop between organisations |
| • Multiple voices confer more credibility with decision makers | • Structures become overly bureaucratic and slow |
| • Larger pool of staff resources to hand | • Lack of clarity about who is doing what |
| • Organisations' different memberships and supporter profiles provide wider spectrum for lobbying | • Members feel inclusion of one/several partners damages joint credibility |
| • Ability to apply pressure at various levels at different times (or at the same time) | • Conflicting positioning (insider/outsider) of organisations leads to watering down of messages to lowest common denominator |
| • Safety in numbers if the issue is controversial | • Larger organisations attract profile |
| • Mutual support during bleak times | • Organisations dispute 'ownership' of funders' leading to funding crisis |
| • Larger organisations can benefit from specialism of smaller organisations | • Not all partners pull their weight |

Many of these, and yet more, difficulties can be overcome; or if they are irresolvable, it may be time to bring collaboration to an end.

During the design and development stage of the campaign cycle, you should look at whether collaboration would help achieve your aim. During the planning stage, you should look at the most appropriate form this collaboration should take. During the implementation stage, you should manage and monitor the collaboration to achieve maximum effectiveness. When evaluations are carried out, you will need to consider how the collaboration contributed to the campaign achieving its outcomes.

## 10.2 How can you work together?

It's important that everyone working together is clear about what collaboration does and doesn't mean. There are many different ways of working together – for example in networks, partnerships, alliances, federations – ranging from very formal structures to very loose, informal arrangements. A useful way of looking at collaboration is to see it as a spectrum, with networks at one end and alliances at the other.

A useful way of looking at collaboration is to see it as a spectrum, with networks at one end and alliances at the other.

### Models of joint working[1]

| Style | Typical Characteristics |
|---|---|
| Networks | A common interest may be the only membership criteria. Usually typified by an informal structure but sometimes has a coordinating secretariat. Often involves regular personal contacts. Emphasis mostly on information and ideas sharing and support rather than joint programmes of work. Members can invest as little as they wish and leave as they wish. |
| Coalitions | Joint working, often among diverse organisations, around a single event, issue or campaign. Members invest significant resources and coordinate their messages, strategies and activities. Different organisations divide the tasks in the most appropriate ways but the structure tends to be formal and requires a high level of trust between participants. Everyone recognises that the coalition has a limited lifetime. |
| Alliances | Long-term, formalised agreement on common ideals among very trusted partners. Very regular consultation between organisations that make a big investment of time in order to make it work. Alliances are usually long-term in nature. Strategies and plans may be jointly developed and implemented. |

If policy makers come to believe that your partnership represents the views of the important players in your specific field of operation then they will come to you for answers and support. For them it is easier to negotiate with one organisation that can deliver a wide spectrum of support than disparate groups of people shouting for their attention.

Seeking to build a partnership of the unexpected directly challenges the 'well they would say that, wouldn't they...' perception.

## The Soil Association

In the early 80s, organic farming was the preserve of a small band of pioneers and was viewed with widespread suspicion and mistrust. Today it is widely accepted as a valid and important contribution to a healthier life and an improved environment. The Soil Association can justifiably claim to have played a key role in this process, having intelligently and intentionally set out to help create, and be part of, a diverse organic movement.

This movement includes farmers, producers and processors who observe the high standards of organic production certified by the Soil Association. Then there are the supermarkets, small retailers and farmers' markets that the Soil Association works with to build a market for organic produce. The Soil Association also plays a role within the environmental movement, lending its authority to issues such as GMOs and intensive farming. And finally, the Soil Association seeks to persuade consumers of the wisdom of purchasing organic produce.

By acting as a link between diverse groups and organisations representing all parts of the supply chain and being therefore perceived to be key cog within a wider movement, the Soil Association is able to speak with great authority to Government. It has helped build powerful partnerships that have made a major contribution to changing agricultural practice in the UK.

Government now publicly states its support for organic farming, organic food is growing in popularity, and the environmental movement promotes the virtues of organic farming.

Remember that collaboration need not only involve organisations and individuals from VCOs. Indeed some of the most successful joint working, which has made the most impact on policy makers, has come from groupings that are unusual in their make up.

This is your chance to think 'outside the box' and to involve other, diverse partners who have the same concern about the problem but who may come from completely different sectors, for example business, youth, local authorities. Seeking to build a partnership of the unexpected directly challenges the 'well they would say that, wouldn't they...' perception.

## Engaging in the debate

When thinking about allies with whom to work in pursuing a campaign aim, it can be tempting to stay within the sector and build a coalition of like-minded VCOs. This can be effective, but policy makers are often looking for wider consensus and the danger of gathering a group of like-minded organisations together is that sometimes the whole doesn't equal more than the sum of its parts.

One striking aspect of the Empty Homes Agency's campaign for compulsory leasing has been the ability to get people on board in the support for changes. This encompassed support from diverse organisations such as the Royal Institution of Chartered Surveyors, the Transport and General Workers Union and the British Property Federation. The range of support from within the property establishment as well as outside gave the campaign significant extra weight and made the Government much more likely to consider that the campaign represented a feasible and reasoned solution to a set of problems it was grappling with within the housing sector.

There is also an expectation that organisations should work together on a common agenda. Targets often find it frustrating to be contacted by a succession of organisations all saying the same thing. There is nothing that is more likely to dissipate any sympathy for your proposition than if there appears to be a lack of coordination for no good reason. People may suspect that your unwillingness to collaborate reveals organisational arrogance, which will do your cause nothing but harm.

Although it is important to be clear what your organisation expects from collaboration, you must recognise that the campaign positioning you have adopted may not be commonly accepted by your desired partners. You need to invest time in developing a shared platform rather than trying to impose your vision.

## 10.3 Managing joint working

It is perhaps inevitable that collaboration will not always run smoothly. People and organisations have different characteristics, may even have competing interests. The structure of your collaboration, though, can help to facilitate communications and minimise the challenges to the group.

Clarity is
needed about
when it is
appropriate
to act as a
member of a
partnership
and when to
act alone.

More often than not, there will be a trade-off to be made
between how quickly you can react to events as a coalition and how
much different participants are involved in decision making. The
demands of collaboration may not be easy to reconcile with the
needs of the campaign. This is why clarity is needed about when it
is appropriate to act as a member of a partnership and when to act
alone. Other members of the coalition should have a common
understanding as to the basis of such decisions. As mentioned
earlier in this book, the policy makers work to their own agenda,
and decisions will not wait for the VCOs' convenience.

---

## Tips for managing collaboration[2]

- Be clear about the campaign focus – a 'framing
  statement' (see Framing the Campaign on page 39) is a
  useful tool to ensure everyone has bought into the same
  campaign concept.
- Set membership criteria and member rights and
  responsibilities; decide who can join. Do you need a
  statement of principles that members sign up to?
- Decide and agree the collaboration's remit – be clear
  about the boundaries of what the collaboration will and
  will not do.
- Agree management structures – who will be on the
  steering committee and what are the criteria for
  membership?  Determine which decisions can be made
  by the steering committee and which need to be referred
  back to wider participation. In larger, more formal
  collaborations, rotating steering committee membership
  may be appropriate to ensure spread of workload and
  also equal input. Are decisions made by consensus or by
  vote and how many organisations need to participate?
- Agree who will contribute which resources, both time
  and physical – this can ensure that everyone contributes
  and nobody feels overburdened. It may be that larger
  organisations can be expected to contribute more.
- Have guidelines for when it is necessary for the
  collaborators to act as a group, with a group identity,
  and when it is appropriate for organisations to act
  individually. Sometimes you will wish to do things alone
  and sometimes in collaboration – it is important to have
  agreed parameters. This is particularly important to
  avoid confusion when approaching the media, opinion
  formers and funders.

> • Decide how you will communicate. Are notes taken at meetings and circulated? How do members stay in touch in an emergency when an immediate response may be required? Where will meetings be held and how often? Will meeting venues rotate, etc?
> • If appropriate, include a time limit for collaboration.
> • Set evaluation parameters and a timetable and mechanisms to review progress at regular intervals (see Section 10.4 below).

## 10.3.1 Getting out what you put in

The degree of benefit from working together tends to increase with the degree of contact and organisation involved. This usually means that there is a trade off between costs and benefits. The more that organisations are prepared to give up their own autonomy and invest time, people and resources in collaboration, the greater the likely increase in recognition and legitimacy for all those involved.

One problem that sometimes arises from this is that individual organisations want to maximise the benefits that they get from working with others whilst minimising the costs to themselves. This can make sustainable, stable collaboration extremely difficult to achieve.

**A model of stable collaboration[3]**

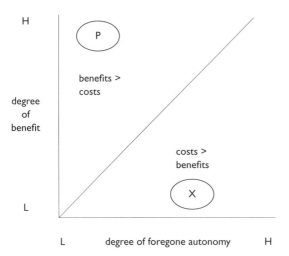

**Judgements should be made early on about the purpose of the collaboration itself (its aim) and the milestones towards achieving this purpose (its objectives).**

The danger in any collaboration is that everyone wants to be at P, reaping the rewards without any cost. But not everyone can be at P and no one wants to be at X. The optimum for the partnership is for everyone to be congregated along the line.

## 10.4 Evaluating collaborative approaches

The same principles that apply to all monitoring and evaluation apply when monitoring and evaluating partnerships: that you should monitor and evaluate progress towards your established objectives and, in doing so, distinguish what you do (outputs) from why you are doing it (outcomes and impact).

When it comes to collaborative approaches within a campaign, it may make sense to think of a monitoring and evaluating system operating along parallel tracks:

1. On one track you are assessing progress towards the campaign aim (see Section 5 as well as the principles and tools outlined in Section 11).
2. On the other, you are assessing progress towards the aim of the collaboration itself.

The implication of this is of course that judgements should be made early on about the purpose of the collaboration itself (its aim) and the milestones towards achieving this purpose (its objectives).

In relation to its overall aim, this can be determined by asking what are the anticipated benefits of the collaboration:

- for the campaign? (some examples of which are outlined in Section 10.1)
- for the participating organisations? (these may include, for example, enhanced profile, improved access to information, efficiency savings, etc.)

In relation to objectives, these should reflect decisions about:

- the set of operating conditions and ways of working that will be needed within your network, coalition or alliance in order for it to be effective in achieving its aims;
- the processes that will be needed, in turn, to achieve them.

Once an aim and objectives are established, indicators and means of verification should be set to assess progress towards them as outlined in Section 5.2.

The monitoring and evaluation framework for the collaboration, in other words, should be developed according to the specific aim and objectives of that particular collaboration and the specific circumstances within which it takes place.

Speaking generally, though, existing thinking suggests that possible areas of investigation could usefully include some of the following:[4]

| | |
|---|---|
| Participation | • How do people participate and at what levels?<br>• What are the trends in participation?<br>• Are people participating as much as they are able to and would like?<br>• Are opportunities provided for participation in decision making and reflection?<br>• What are the obstacles to participation and what can be done about them? |
| Trust | • What is the level of trust between participants? And between participants and the secretariat, if there is one?<br>• How do participants perceive levels of trust to have changed over time?<br>• What mechanisms are in place to enable trust to flourish? How might these be strengthened? |
| Diversity and dynamism | • How easy is it for members to contribute their ideas and follow through on them?<br>• How far does the collaboration reach? Is this as broad as intended? Is it too broad for the work you are trying to do? |
| Democracy | • What are the power relationships? How do the powerful and less powerful inter-relate?<br>• Who sets the objectives, has access to the resources, participates in the governance?<br>• Is there a good balance between consensus-building and action?<br>• What kind of mechanisms are in place to facilitate the resolution of conflicts? |
| Political accountability within the campaign[5] | • Do participants' objectives interlock?<br>• Is there continuous joint review of strategy?<br>• Is information easily accessible and freely shared amongst participants?<br>• Are any risk assessments based upon the effects on the most vulnerable? |
| Leadership and sustainability | • Are the goals of the partnership clear and common?<br>• Are structures financially and operationally sustainable?<br>• Is the structure appropriate for the work of the partnership?<br>• Where are most decisions taken?<br>• Is leadership facilitative?<br>• Is the level of contribution from, and benefit to, different participants a stable one? (NB one way to test this would be for organisations to plot where they perceive themselves on the 'P/X' graph in Section 10.3.1). |

**The monitoring and evaluation framework for the collaboration should be developed according to the specific aim and objectives of that particular collaboration and the specific circumstances within which it takes place.**

**It is necessary to have a common vision of how the collaboration will work and understanding of what organisations seek to gain from the collaboration.**

Although this section has concentrated on the pitfalls and difficulties of campaigning together, it is our contention that organisations should, wherever possible, seek to work together as collaboration often increases the likelihood of impact.

But, from the outset, it is also necessary to have a common vision of how the collaboration will work and a common and openly stated understanding of what organisations seek to gain from the collaboration.

## Learning points

You may wish to consider the following:

✓ Collaboration with other organisations will almost always strengthen your campaign but all participants need to have a common understanding about the purpose and parameters of joint campaign activity.

✓ Have you identified the anticipated benefits of collaboration and weighed up the possible cost at an early stage?

✓ Is there clarity around when it is appropriate to act as a member of a partnership and when to act alone?

✓ Are you monitoring and evaluating the effectiveness of the partnership as well as your progress towards the campaign objectives?

1. adapted from Chapman, J and Wameyo, A (2001) *Monitoring and Evaluating Advocacy: A scoping study*. Action Aid and
   Cohen, D, de la Vega, R and Watson, G (2001) Advocacy for Social Justice: A Global Action and Reflection Guide. Kumarian Press Inc.
2. adapted from Vaneklasen, L with Miller, V (2002) *A new weave of power, people and politics: The action guide for advocacy & citizen participation*. World Neighbors
3. Fowler, A (1997) *Striking a Balance: A Guide to Enhancing the Effectiveness of Non Governmental Organisations in International Development*. Earthscan
4. questions taken in particular from Church, M et al (2003) *Participation, relationships and Dynamic Change: New Thinking on Evaluating the Work of International Networks*. Development Planning Unit, University College London, especially the checklist pp54-55
5. this row of table taken from van Tujil, P and Jordan, L (1999) *Political Responsibility in Transnational NGO Advocacy*. Bank Information Center, Washington DC

# 11 | Monitoring and evaluating campaigns

*"If it quacks and has feathers, it's probably a duck."*
**proverb**

## 11.1 Some principles in monitoring and evaluation

Although monitoring and evaluation is an accepted part of best practice in other fields (such as service delivery and fundraising), people often believe that it is inherently unfeasible to assess campaigns in a similar way.

It is true that there are some complications specific to evaluating campaigns. Reviewing social and political change, and analysing the factors that influence it, can be complex. But these difficulties can be overcome. And it makes no sense not to try to monitor and evaluate your work because it is only by doing so that you can learn from mistakes and experiences, and improve the way you and others campaign.

A monitoring and evaluation framework has already been set out in Section 5.2. This section now explores some of the issues relating to monitoring and evaluation in more depth. It outlines a set of suggested principles for thinking about and adopting a learning-based approach and identifies some tools to take this approach forward.

### Start with clarity of purpose

As already explained, this book maintains that one of the first rules of campaigning is to be clear about what it is exactly that you are trying to achieve – what is your aim and what are your objectives?

Our experience is that the problems that people claim to have with monitoring and evaluating campaigns can often be traced

**Problems that people claim to have with monitoring and evaluating campaigns can often be traced back to problems that are actually to do with planning.**

back to problems that are actually to do with planning. Unless you start with a clear aim and achievable objectives against which to measure campaign progress, evaluation is likely to prove problematic.

### A role for aspiration

There is a tendency amongst campaigners to set over-ambitious objectives.

The problem with this is that it reduces accountability and makes conclusions about campaign effectiveness very difficult to reach.

One way to deal with this in planning is to recognise a distinction between the (publicly asserted) purpose of the campaign and the campaign objectives (for internal use only). The publicly stated purpose of the campaign may be bold and ambitious to help give the campaign momentum – this is the place for aspiration. But the internally stated objectives should always be realistic, so that progress towards them can reasonably be assessed.

It may be helpful here to think of a planning hierarchy shaping your campaigning programme, incorporating both bold vision (at the top) and hard-headed reality (towards the bottom) at different levels of a planning pyramid:

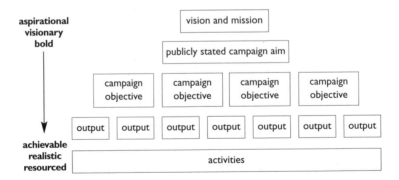

It may be better that your campaign target is unaware of your internal objectives because then they will know that your publicly stated purpose is essentially a lever to achieve less aspirational objectives.

## Allocate the necessary resources

If you can find money to run a campaign, appropriate resources for monitoring and evaluation should also be made available. As a small organisation, it is possible to conduct evaluations simply and cheaply. As a larger organisation, you can do it in more sophisticated ways. Either way, as long as the appropriate resources are invested in evaluation, you will learn from the experience.

Indeed funders should expect you to demonstrate that your campaign is to be assessed and provision should be made in funding bids for monitoring and evaluating your campaigning activity.

**As long as the appropriate resources are invested in evaluation, you will learn from the experience.**

## Look for evidence not proof

Social and political change is complex and multidirectional. Trying to prove causal links between campaign activities and certain social transformations ignores this complexity.

Best practice suggests therefore that you should not look for proof but instead seek to build the evidence that could reasonably be used to assert a connection between your activities and subsequent social and political change.

In most cases, you don't need to perform a forensic autopsy. If it quacks and has feathers, it's probably a duck.

## Build a critical mass of information

The best way to build the evidence you need is through pulling together a 'critical mass' of information. It's very unlikely that any one indicator or one view will be sufficient to demonstrate the effects of a particular campaign. A better approach is to build and present a range of evidence which, taken together, offers more than the sum of its parts.

**Build and present a range of evidence which, taken together, offers more than the sum of its parts.**

## Measure the important things not the easy things

Our experience is that in campaigning there is still a tendency to focus on activities and outputs (the number of launches, events, letters, etc.) rather than outcomes (what happened because of this activity).

This is understandable; after all, outputs are easier to measure, more easily quantifiable and more clearly within the control of the campaign. The danger, however, is that overemphasising the measurement of outputs can have a distorting effect on the campaign itself.

This is because of the reality that 'what gets measured gets done'. There are countless examples in all sorts of situations of how the setting of objectives leads to effort being redirected to achieve them. That's why in setting objectives and monitoring and evaluating progress, you need to focus on the important things.

Campaign evaluations should concentrate on the key questions:
- Has there been change over time?
- How significant was the change?
- Was the change intended or not?
- Was it change for the better?
- What made it happen?

### Keep it simple and user friendly

Monitoring and evaluation based on too many indicators usually proves to be counter-productive because it can end up being both time-consuming and too diverting. The ideal is to develop a small number of indicators that substantively capture changes in the situation. A system for monitoring these indicators needs to be built into the campaign plan.

It's important too that the things being measured have some value to the people who are actually doing the measuring. If they don't see the point, the information you get from them is liable to be incomplete and inaccurate. Decisions on what to collect, when to collect it, how to record it and how to use it should therefore be taken in consultation – as far as possible – with those who will be responsible for collecting it.

### Use comparative data

Monitoring and evaluating campaigns is about measuring change over time. Because of this, baseline research can be very helpful in informing future assessments. Baseline data (gathered before the campaign launch) provide a guide, a snapshot of the issue in a historical context, against which all subsequent progress can be measured. Without it, it can be even more difficult to disentangle results and ascribe outcomes to the particular campaign.

Where baseline data do not exist, as a substitute it may be possible to try to build a picture using retrospective questions such as 'how did you feel/what did you think before x?'.

Similarly, use of control groups (where responses of people who have been exposed to the campaign are compared with responses of those who have not) can isolate the variables and thus help in being able to attribute changes to the campaign activity. However, this approach may not always be desirable (you may not want to exclude groups from the campaign just for the sake of being able to evaluate it better) or even possible (for example because existing dissimilarities between different groups before your intervention took place may also be difficult to avoid).

**Be responsive**

It is also likely that there will be unexpected outcomes of your campaign. Your evaluation framework should be sufficiently flexible so that interesting or unexpected developments can be incorporated within it (see also Section 9.6.2). In particular, it is often the case that it becomes apparent that outcomes set at the beginning represent too narrow a conception of the changes actually being brought about.

In other words, be prepared to look beyond the indicators determined at the start of the campaign, making explicit the rationale for any changes that you subsequently introduce.

Your campaign may be focused on securing institutional change, or changes in people's behaviour. But there may well be other areas in which your campaign will be having an effect, and these are legitimate areas for consideration too in any review of the changes that your intervention has helped generate.

> Be prepared to look beyond the indicators determined at the start of the campaign.

---

### Adapting objectives

In a recent campaign Drugscope originally set objectives around media coverage and influencing the terms of the debate on women/drugs/prison. They subsequently found that one of the key results of the campaign was in developing new contacts for the organisation, which were of value not only for the campaign but also for future organisational work. This unplanned-for outcome was incorporated within the framework of their campaign evaluation.

---

**Integrate monitoring and evaluation**

As well as integrating monitoring and evaluation within the campaign cycle, it may also be necessary to ensure that the monitoring and evaluation meshes with wider organisational systems, such as performance appraisal processes.

**You need to reject the idea of a single reality. Evaluation is never neutral, even within an organisation of two people.**

In assessing its work, the organisation as a whole needs to consider the impact that its work is having. To do this effectively, it makes sense if individual departments and disciplines feed into a common approach but also take lead responsibility for what lies within their remit. To take one example, if there is a separate policy research team, from whom the campaigners take the policy change aims, then the objective of the campaigners should reasonably be to get that change effected. If the policy change is achieved and it doesn't have the desired impact, responsibility for this does not lie with the campaigners who have achieved their objective.

### Get the right levels of participation

Campaign evaluation is ultimately a matter of subjective judgement.

The key question is not only 'what has changed?' but also, 'what happened to effect those changes?'. This involves questions about the relative significance of different interventions. Who decides this can be critical, because there are likely to be widely different views, especially in campaigning where outright victory is rare. Compromise is often the result.

Who decides whether the result was a noble gain or a sellout? Were small gains consistent with the wider objectives of the campaign, or was the campaign co-opted? There are likely to be a variety of opinions among different partners and stakeholders in a campaign.

You need to reject the idea of a single reality. Evaluation is never neutral, even within an organisation of two people.

That's why there need to be checks and balances in place in the monitoring and evaluation system to ensure there is input from multiple sources. Issues of participation are complicated but a reasonable summary is that you need to consider carefully who should be involved in an evaluation, how and when.

---

## Who should participate?

Think about the appropriate participation of the following audiences:[1]
- intended beneficiaries
- those who have been working on the issue within (and in partnership with) your organisation, including local community organisations and groups;
- decision makers and officials;

---

- journalists;
- academics;
- wider public audiences;
- donors;
- non-stakeholders (i.e. those who have not been involved in the work you are assessing) – e.g. as a control group (against which to measure what's changed because of your work rather than because of other developments that would have led to the changes anyway).

One thing to avoid is the over-reliance on internal information and internal perspectives.

For the same reason that others are likely to over-emphasise their role in any change, you could very easily end up doing the same. Gathering information from multiple perspectives through widespread participation helps eliminate this kind of bias in your findings.

Obviously there will be questions that can best be answered internally, for example about how resources were managed and how well processes worked. But, thinking back to the impact chain, as a rule of thumb, the further towards impact your enquiries lean, the less the evaluation should rely on internally generated information and the more it should incorporate external perspectives:

## (Simplified) balancing of inputs within monitoring and evaluation

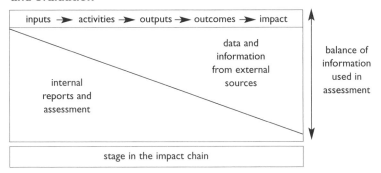

### External evaluations

In some cases, it will be important that the evaluation be carried out by people who have no stake in the results of the evaluation. This may be simply because funders require it or because individuals who have been tasked with delivering objectives are likely to find it difficult to judge (or get reliable feedback from others on) their own performance.

In these cases, it may be preferable for an evaluation to be carried out by someone external to the campaign team, possibly even someone from outside your organisation.

Whether the evaluation is conducted internally, or you bring in external experts, or there is a mix of approaches, there is a balancing act to perform between the organisational need honestly to learn the lessons from experience and the desire to show achievements to stakeholders such as donors.

The point is the need to be open to criticism, understanding that funders increasingly respect transparency and suspect whitewash.

**Funders increasingly respect transparency and suspect whitewash.**

### Give feedback

Findings should be visible and accessible, allowing audiences to see progress towards (or deviation from) the campaign objectives and aim. Records and reports need to recognise that different people have different needs, and reports on progress should be tailored to those needs.

---

### Feedback

A number of groups with an interest in the campaign require feedback; each has different requirements, entailing distinct strategies. Think about the best ways of feeding back to the following audiences:
- intended beneficiaries
- trustees
- senior managers
- staff
- volunteers
- committed activists and campaign supporters
- other supporters, such as donors
- media
- politicians
- organisations you are working with
- the wider public

---

As part of the monitoring and evaluation framework, organisations need to create capacity to fulfil these different information needs. Part of this is about simplifying the information in ways that don't eliminate meaning.

---

### Objectives rating system: an example of how to present simplified information[2]

This reporting system involves rating progress against objectives using a simple scoring system, where the score reflects the amount of progress made.

For outcomes there is a four-point rating system where:
1 = significant change towards objective compared to baseline situation
2 = positive change towards objective compared to baseline situation
3 = unchanged – no perceptible change between baseline and objective
4 = negative change – reversal to a level below the baseline

For outputs there is a three-point rating system reflecting the degree to which an output's targets have been met where:
1 = no change on baseline where the output had not been met
2 = partial movement towards achieving the output
3 = output achieved

These data, along with the relevant amount of background explanation, may provide a brief and easily digestible snapshot of progress.

---

**Evaluate campaign processes as well as outcomes**

In addition to thinking about outcomes, the delivery of the campaign should itself be periodically considered.

This would ideally involve both:
- a review of campaign actions to see whether plans have been delivered according to budget, accounting for discrepancies
- assessment of the extent to which ways of working facilitate or hamper effective campaign delivery

It makes
sense to
focus on and
measure
things that
the organisa-
tion seeks to
value.

### 11.1.1 Campaign action

The question here is relatively simple: have activities been delivered according to the plan?

How this question breaks down depends on the nature of the specific campaign but might include for example a review of:
- whether available research had been presented clearly and persuasively
- whether events ran smoothly and successfully
- whether accounting procedures are adequate.

### 11.1.2 Campaign ways of working

It makes sense to focus on and measure things that the organisation seeks to value. As an example,[3] this might include questions about:

- how planning and management structures and processes encourage flexibility
- how, through planning and management, innovation is promoted
- the extent to which the campaign is focused on external audiences rather than internal bureaucracy
- how campaigners' skills have been enhanced.

### Who's winning

One final area can get lost in functional reviews of progress and processes but might be said to be the most important of all: who's winning the campaign?

Are you inspired and motivated to keep on? Or are you or your organisation or your network disappointed, overwhelmed or discouraged by progress so far?

If it's the latter, how can you turn the tables? How can the campaign be reinvigorated?

### Do it

There are many concerns expressed by campaigners about, for example, the cost (in time and money) of evaluation and the difficulties of attribution.

These concerns can be addressed within a carefully constructed evaluation framework. What any such framework does not counter, however, is that reluctance to carry out evaluations is often due to a culture within campaigning that values activism over reflection and leaves campaigners running from one campaign to another with massive workloads and no time to focus on why they are doing what they are doing.

*It should be okay to make a mistake, but not to keep making the same mistake.*

This approach risks missing not only the point of monitoring and evaluation but also the point about campaigning which is that it should be okay to make a mistake, but not to keep making the same mistake.

What this means for monitoring and evaluation is that you should carry it out as well as you can in the circumstances and then learn from your experiences.

## 11.2 A note on measuring and evaluation tools and techniques

Below are some approaches that can be adopted according to the specific campaign context. As already noted, in most cases, tools and techniques would be used in combination, not in isolation.

### 11.2.1 Proxy measures of change

Evaluations need to record progress towards the campaign's objectives and aim: this should normally mean focusing attention on measuring progress against outcomes (as opposed to outputs).

*Evaluations need to record progress towards the campaign's objectives and aim.*

There will, however, be cases where outcomes may be difficult to measure directly and/or difficult to attribute to the campaign. Or it simply may not be cost-effective to measure the outcome directly. If, for example, you are a small organisation running a campaign, a small part of which involves trying to promote your issue in the media and into the public domain more generally, it probably won't make sense to spend time and money trying to measure any public reaction to this coverage.

In situations such as this, it may make sense to establish what are called 'proxy measures of change'. Measurements, in other words, of aspects of the campaign that, if delivered, may be safely assumed to have a link with, or lead to, the desired outcomes.

At one level, this could involve focusing on measuring outputs and their short-term results. This would probably involve, for example a quantitative review of how messages have been disseminated and promoted. How much press coverage did you get? How many hits on your campaign website? This can be done relatively easily through media tracking, website monitoring, etc.

It makes sense to think about measuring these outputs in slightly more meaningful ways by incorporating qualitative assessments. For example when looking at local press coverage, take into account:

- whether coverage is in target media
- how prominent it is
- how positively it reflects on the organisational view of the issue
- whether key phrases, or accurate quotations, are used.

From these kinds of approaches, perhaps backed by additional audience research, it is possible to gather information that provides evidence of:

- campaign coverage (total audience reached);
- recognition of campaign messages (in answer to the question, 'have you seen this before?');
- spontaneous campaign message recall (where your messages are correctly linked to your organisation and your campaign without prompting);
- the extent to which the message is believed by those hearing it to be credible and relevant;
- audiences' intention to take a particular action as a result.

These are proxy measures, because they don't represent evidence of actual change, but, in combination, it may be reasonable to put a case that if these things are achieved, then it's likely that actual change will result.

This information also provides useful evidence for reviewing the existing campaign or improving future campaigns, helping to answer key questions such as:

- Have the people who were supposed to hear your messages heard them?
- If not, how can you better reach these audiences?
- How were your messages interpreted by those who heard them?
- Did your audiences respond positively to your messages?
- Which messages worked? Why?
- Which did not work? Why?
- How can you alter the messages that were not effective?
- How were your messages differentiated from those of others?
- Which techniques of delivery worked well?
- Which were not effective and why? How can these techniques be changed or improved?
- Was media/press coverage helpful to your effort?
- How could your media relations be improved?[4]

### 11.2.2 Multiple appraisal

This technique involves gathering information from key players at all stages in the campaign influencing process, from staff internally and partners and allies, to journalists, officials, MPs and other interested parties. The results can be amalgamated as an aggregate of informed views about the effectiveness of the campaign, and its effects.

This kind of review would normally best be conducted by external evaluators, in order to encourage candour and maximise objectivity. Information garnered in this way would best be used in tandem with other information sources (e.g. quantitative and qualitative research, see Section 12.4.3).

Additional information can be gained from the fact that it is likely that there will be a number of informal comments made about the campaign. There will probably be times when some aspect of the campaign is cited, in either positive or negative ways, by the campaign target or others involved in it in some way.

All this helps to build an overall picture of the campaign's influence, and monitoring systems should be in place to capture these kinds of comments, and maybe even to seek them out.

**One of the tasks facing the campaigner is to present the issue in a way that is more reflective of the worldview the campaign is trying to promote.**

### 11.2.3 Framing analysis

In Section 4.3, it was explained that all issues are 'framed' in some way, normally in ways that suit dominant interests.

In many cases, one of the tasks facing the campaigner is to present the issue in a way that is more reflective of the worldview the campaign is trying to promote. In other words, to reframe the issue.

Framing analysis is a way of reviewing progress of the campaign by examining how the issue is framed, and how this changes over time:

| how is the issue generally framed in: | at the beginning of the campaign | at end of period x | at end of period y |
|---|---|---|---|
| the tabloids | | | |
| the broadcast media | | | |
| the broadsheets/ | | | |
| compacts | | | |
| public debate and discourse | | | |
| policy debate and discourse | | | |
| other relevant forums | | | |

As well as looking at the ways in which the issue is described, other possible areas worthy of exploration within this kind of analysis might include the extent to which there is:

- expanded dialogue and debate;
- increased accuracy in the way that the issue is represented;
- increased incidence of the people centrally affected by the issue being given an opportunity to voice their perspective in the debate and dialogue;
- an enhanced sense that the issue resonates with people's everyday interests.[5]

### 11.2.4 Tracking surveys

This technique involves tracking target audiences' responses to a campaign through longitudinal research (i.e. repeated surveys) and seeking evidence of change relating, for example, to levels of campaign message recognition and recall.

For more on research, see Section 12.

### 11.2.5 Theory-based approaches

All campaigns operate based on some kind of 'theory of change'.

In other words, every campaign is run based on a set of assumptions as to:

- how social and political change happens; and
- how that particular campaign is going to have an influence on these processes.

All campaigns work to a theory of change whether the theory, and the assumptions behind it, is made explicit or not. Our experience is that the assumptions underpinning campaigns about how change happens are not always sufficiently thought through.

This book began by talking about the impact chain as a valuable tool in deconstructing how change happens. It is suggested (in Part Five) that making the theory of change explicit and examining its validity can be a helpful way of making a campaign more robust and more focused. In Part Five, a number of specific models of change are posited and each of these can be used in monitoring and evaluation.

In each of the different cases cited, this kind of modelling offers a framework within which to assess how a particular campaign has affected (or not) the campaign target and others the campaign seeks to influence or engage.

## Learning points

You may wish to consider the following:

- ✓ Monitoring and evaluating campaigns will help ensure that current campaigning activity is well directed and that lessons are learned for future campaigning. Remember to plan for it and do it.
- ✓ Are you clear about your aims and objectives?
- ✓ Are resources allocated for monitoring and evaluation?
- ✓ Can you build and present a range of evidence?
- ✓ Do your indicators substantively capture changes in the situation?
- ✓ Can you involve those who will be collecting information in key decisions on what to collect?
- ✓ Have you considered unexpected outcomes as well as those that are planned for?
- ✓ Can monitoring and evaluation be integrated not only into the campaign cycle but also the wider organisational systems?
- ✓ Are your findings visible and accessible?
- ✓ Are you evaluating the campaign processes as well as the outcomes?

1. Roche, C (1999) *Impact Assessment for Development Agencies: Learning to Value Change*. Oxfam
2. adapted from United Nations Development Programme Evaluation Office (2002) *Handbook on Monitoring and Evaluating for Results*. UNDP
3. borrowing from Peters, T (1998) *Thriving on Chaos: Handbook for a Management Revolution*. Macmillan London
4. adapted from Sharma, R R (1999) *An Introduction to Advocacy: Training Guide*. SARA/AED
5. Rockefeller Foundation Communication and Social Change Network (2001) *Measuring and Evaluating Communication for Social Change*. Communication Initiative Forum

# 12 Organising campaign intelligence

*"T'Aint what you do it's the way that you do it,*
*T'Aint what you do it's the time that you do it,*
*T'Aint what you do it's the place that you do it*
*And that's what gets results!"*
**Sy Oliver & James "Trummy" Young**

## 12.1 Having a campaign intelligence system – the rationale

Good intelligence is vital to any campaign. Campaigns should be based on research not assumptions – knowledge not guesswork.

As argued in Part Two, having the right kind of intelligence involves being properly informed about three key areas, and how they affect your campaign. These are:
1. the issue
2. the campaigning environment
3. the internal context

Top quality information in these three areas is needed to inform campaign design, development and planning. It is also needed so that you can respond to changes in the situation (through monitoring) and review progress (through evaluation). Developing a good campaign intelligence system is therefore about meeting the information needs of the campaign you are currently engaged in.

But it is also important to think beyond the information needs of the specific campaign. A sound intelligence system is also valuable for the wider campaigning programme – without a good intelligence system, organisations have no institutional memory. This means that the same lessons are re-learned again and again and sometimes even again! This is usually revealed when

**Campaigns should be based on research not assumptions.**

**Developing a good campaign intelligence system is about meeting the information needs of the campaign.**

campaigning staff or volunteers leave. It is discovered that the information they held in their heads was valuable intelligence and that the organisation has no formal record of it.

The purpose of developing a campaign intelligence system is to help you focus on the core information needed to progress the campaign and the campaigning programme, and help identify how, and when, this information is going to be needed. It ensures that you collect and record the right quantity of information. You should not waste time collecting information that will never be needed. Similarly, you should not have to waste time relearning basic information because it has never been recorded.

Too little or too much information are twin evils in campaigning. Too little information and the basis on which you make decisions about your campaign may well turn out to be flawed. But equally, it is easy to be overwhelmed by information that may not be relevant to helping your campaigning effectiveness.

## Building a coherent approach

Elements within the NSPCC's approach towards monitoring and evaluating campaign progress include the following strands:

(a) authoritative baseline research (i.e. prior to the launch of the campaign) incorporating:
- policy research
- evidence of public attitudes towards child abuse and towards the NSPCC itself

In both cases, evidence gathered has been used both to inform the evolving campaign and to enable future judgements about what has changed as a result of the NSPCC's interventions.

(b) longitudinal research with public audiences, tracking attitudes and behaviour measures, over time; such people's:
- awareness of child abuse
- assessment of the relative importance of issues of child abuse
- recognition of different issues as constituting abuse
- preparedness to act in response to perceived abuse

(c) more targeted longitudinal research focused on key audiences whom the campaign seeks to influence/engage,

gathering evidence of recollection of messages, perceptions of effectiveness of delivery, etc., from target groups including:
- MPs
- journalists
- the NSPCC's own donors

(d) data and information capturing the volume and quality of media coverage by campaign, by region, and by audience.

(e) specific research to test the resonance of particular high profile campaigning, such as TV advertising, so as to be able to assess the correlation between major effort and subsequent result and to investigate whether audiences get the specific point of a particular campaign as well as the more general messages.

Taken together, this research is providing the NSPCC with vital intelligence to assist in:
- assessing how well its campaign messages are being disseminated and assimilated;
- judging the relative effectiveness of different campaigning techniques and actions and reacting accordingly;
- identifying and targeting the people who are more likely to act and be advocates for the NSPCC's campaign aims;
- shaping the development of the campaigning programme – the focus of the recent 'Someone To Turn To' campaign, for example, is to make it easier for people to report abuse, an initiative partly informed by findings from marketing research;
- making judgements about, and being accountable for, the ways that it is using its overall resources.

The NSPCC's campaigning is well resourced in comparison to many and so the degree of sophistication and coherence of this approach may not always be appropriate. But one thing that is replicable is the principle that a proportion of the campaign budget (in the NSPCC's case around six per cent) should be dedicated to monitoring and evaluation. Any organisation in any circumstances can gather information that will be useful to its campaigning through dedicating a similar proportion of the budget to research.

## 12.2 Campaign intelligence systems – starting out

One first step in developing a campaign intelligence system is to answer the following questions:
- what are the important decisions needed as the campaign progresses?
- what information is needed to help make these decisions?
- what is known already?
- what are the best ways to find out what isn't known?
- what resources are there to find this out?
- what is the benefit of this information and does it outweigh the cost, in terms of time, effort and money, of finding it out?

In this section, we considered ways in which it might be possible to think systematically about the information you need and how to get it.

One way to do this is through the development of an integrated campaign intelligence system that links:
1. what information is needed (see Section 12.2 below)
2. how to gather the information (see Section 12.3)
3. how to manage the information (see Section 12.4)

The information that is needed in relation to the issue, the campaigning environment and the internal context has already been identified. You will gain this information from a combination of secondary and primary data:
- primary data = data especially collected through your own research
- secondary data = information that is already available elsewhere

There are four main means of gathering the range of primary and secondary data needed; these are:
- scanning for information
- policy research
- marketing research
- internal reports

Taken together, these elements can combine to form a campaign intelligence system that looks something like this:

## Campaign intelligence system components[1]

```
                    ┌──────────────────────┐
                    │      THE ISSUE       │◄─────────────┐
                    │ problems and solutions│              │
                    └──────────────────────┘              │
                              │                           │
                              ▼                           │
                    ┌──────────────────────┐              │
                    │    THE CAMPAIGN      │              │
                    │ INTELLIGENCE SYSTEM  │              │
          ┌────────►│      scanning        │              │
          │         │   policy research    │              │
          │         │   market research    │              │
          │         │  internal reporting  │──────┐       │
          │         └──────────────────────┘      ▼       │
  ┌───────────────┐         ▲          ┌──────────────────┐
  │THE CAMPAIGNING│         │          │  MANAGING THE    │
  │  ENVIRONMENT  │         │          │    CAMPAIGN      │
  │  the target   │         │          │    planning      │
  │the routes of  │ ┌───────────────┐  │implementation and│
  │  influence    │ │INTERNAL CONTEXT│ │   monitoring     │
  │other key      │ │ strengths and │  │   evaluation     │
  │ stakeholders  │ │  weaknesses   │  └──────────────────┘
  │public audiences│ │campaign techniques│        │
  │the wider      │ └───────────────┘            │
  │ campaigning   │         ▲                    │
  │ environment   │         │                    │
  └───────────────┘         │                    │
          ▲                 │                    │
          └─────────────────┴────────────────────┘
```

## 12.3 What information is needed

In Section 3, some key questions were identified to explore in the campaign development phase in relation to the issue and the context, and tools (such as the problem and solution tree) were introduced as a way of ordering that information. We now suggest that you build on this approach to develop a systematic approach to managing information. It is likely that the same kinds of questions asked at the beginning will also need to be asked for the duration of the campaign, and at the end, in evaluation (see fig overleaf).

The trick is to identify the key questions and then invest the resources to be able to answer each question with the minimal amount of effort to the right level of detail. The point is that you should always be able to identify the answers to the questions in the figure below (or your own version) to the requisite amount of precision and accuracy.

How up to date this information will need to be depends on the specific question and the particular nature of the campaign and campaigning programme. Some things will probably need to be continually tracked to ensure information is always to hand, for example, the stance of the target and key routes of influence on the issue. Other aspects of the intelligence system may require only periodic or one-off assessments, for example, an internal review of structure may have to happen only once every few years (if at all).

| | Stage in campaign | | |
| --- | --- | --- | --- |
| | design, development and planning | implementation and monitoring | evaluation |
| **The issue**<br>• what are the problems?<br>• what are their causes?<br>• what are their effects?<br>• what are the potential solutions?<br>• which solution are you focusing on?<br>• what personal testimonies can be used to illustrate the problem/the campaign? | ✓ | ✓ | ✓ |
| **The campaign environment**<br>• who are the key players (i.e. who is the target and what are the primary routes of influence)?<br>• how much influence do they each have?<br>• what is their stance on the issue?<br>• how important do they believe the issue to be?<br>• how susceptible are they to influence?<br>• how can the campaign best influence them?<br>• what wider trends are affecting the campaign environment? | ✓ | ✓ | ✓ |
| **The internal context**<br>• do you have clarity of purpose?<br>• do you have the necessary resources, skills and expertise?<br>• do you have legitimacy to speak on the issue and the credibility to do so with authority?<br>• are you accountable to stakeholders?<br>• is your organisation oriented in ways that enable effective campaigning? | ✓ | ✓ | ✓ |

## 12.4 Gathering the information

### 12.4.1 Scanning

The best place to start when identifying sources of information is usually with secondary data. It may well prove expensive and time consuming to do the research yourself so you should look first to see what information already exists. If the information is available, you need to take into account that people produce and disseminate research for all kinds of reasons and with different motives, so you need to be sure of its origin and reliability before you use secondary research without qualification.

Various sources are available to you. Below is a checklist, but it is not definitive and you should develop your own scanning systems. Be thankful that you live in the age of the internet; gathering the information is now far simpler if you have access to the technology. Even if you don't you should be able to find the information by using libraries or by contacting people who can answer your questions.

> **You need to take into account that people produce and disseminate research for all kinds of reasons and with different motives.**

> **Government**
> - Which government ministers have responsibility or interests in your area of work? (see www.parliament.uk/directories/directories.cfm)
> - Do they have constituency interests, personal interests, a track record as an ally or an opponent? What support have they shown in public statements, transcripts of speeches, in their voting record on relevant issues, or in response to Parliamentary debate and to your own supporters' correspondence?
> - Which government departments are relevant to your work? Who are the relevant officials and what is policy on your issue? (see www.number10.gov.uk/output/page30.asp)
> - Can you arrange for regular information into/feedback from the relevant departments, e.g. does it have a voluntary sector working group/consultations/subject advisory groups?
>
> **Parties**
> - Is Labour Party policy positive towards your issue? If not can it be influenced through the National Policy Forum or the Joint Policy Committee (see www.labour.org.uk/policyforum/)

- What is the Conservative Party position on your issue? (www.conservatives.com)
- What is the Liberal Democrat position on your issue? (www.libdems.org.uk/index.cfm/page.main/section.policy)
- Are there other minority parties with specialist interest in the issue?

### Parliament
- Which Select Committees are relevant for your work? (Commons and Lords) (see www.parliament.uk/parliamentarycommittees/background.cfm)
- Who are the Members and what is their stance on the issue?
- When does the Committee meet, what enquiries are planned, how you can submit or give evidence?
- Who administers the Committee? What is their background and what views have they expressed in public on your issue?
- How is legislation made – e.g. what is the Parliamentary timetable, what are the opportunities for asking questions or initiating debates?
- Which other MPs' Groups or Committees affect your work, e.g. All Party Groups (MPs and Peers), Labour Party Departmental Committees, opposition party structures and groups?
- Who are the key opposition spokespeople for your issue? What is their stance on your issue?

### European Union (EU) Institutions
- Is your issue affected by the EU?

Nolan Quigley, NCVO's European and International Officer says, "An estimated 60 to 80 per cent of new legislation now originates in the European Union. Many English voluntary sector organisations have been campaigning at the EU level for some time and have achieved some significant successes. Finding your way around the various processes and institutions can be a daunting prospect, especially at the beginning. So what do the EU institutions actually do? The European Commission (see www.europa.eu.int/comm/index_en.htm) is both the EU's executive which drafts proposed new European laws on its own initiative, and at the same time it is also the EU's civil service, checking that member states correctly implement EU laws and supervising how EU funds are spent. The European Parliament is growing in power and influence and MEPs can and do table amendments which make real changes to EU laws. The Parliament's committees are where the serious amendments happen, so choosing an MEP on a relevant committee is key to any successful campaign. (See www.europarl.eu.int for a full list of committees and members.) Finally, the Council of Ministers, (see www.consilium.eu.int) made up of sitting ministers from all of the EU's member states, brings the national perspectives to the process, so any campaigning at the Council of Ministers would actually take place in the national capitals. Networks and umbrella organisations are in place across the EU to help make campaigning and coalition-building at the EU level, a realistic proposition for organisations of whatever size. To find out more about how it all works and a few tips on where to start, NCVO has prepared a guide, 'How to campaign at the EU level? A Guide from NCVO.' Go to www.ncvo-vol.org.uk/eurocampaign.

**Other relevant institutions**
- Is your issue affected by the work of the National Assembly for Wales (see www.wales.gov.uk/index.htm), the Scottish Parliament (see www.scottish.parliament.uk) or the Northern Ireland Assembly (see www.niassembly.gov.uk)? If so, which committees are relevant to you, who are the members and what is their stance on your issue? How will you stay updated on enquiries and progress of legislation? Can you use these as influencing routes to central government?
- Do regional and local government affect your work? For a list of regional government structures and offices, see www.odpm.gov.uk (follow links to regions). For information on the Greater London Authority and its work see www.london.gov.uk and for general issues and news affecting local authorities in general see www.info4local.gov.uk. Find out what routes exist to raise concerns regarding your issue, from regional or local government to central government.
- Are there semi-autonomous or autonomous bodies inputting to policy formulation that are relevant to your work, e.g. government commissions, agencies?

**Media and public audiences**
- How much of an issue is it? How much coverage does it get in the media?
- How does the issue tend to be 'framed' in the media?
- Which journalists take an interest in the issue and what is their stance on it?
- What do public audiences think about the issue? Is there any existing relevant market research (e.g. at www.mori.co.uk)?
- What do they know about your organisation?

**The wider campaigning environment**
- What's going on in the world of campaigning? What innovations are occurring? Who's being successful? What are they doing? (see for example www.thirdsector.co.uk/home/index.cfm or society.guardian.co.uk/voluntary/ or www.voluntarysector.co.uk)
- What is the funding environment for campaigning and how is it changing?
- How are the national/regional/local/international policy-making environments changing?
- What are the key political developments (e.g. national elections, UK Presidency of the EU, local elections in England, regional government establishment, elections for mayors?)
- What other key trends and changes (e.g. in volunteering, charity legislation, technology) are affecting the ways that people react to and get involved in your campaigning?

### 12.4.2 Policy research

It is important that you seek to collect information that shows the campaign to be credible and also for staff to gain a grasp of the issue. For this, it is likely that you will need:
- evidence that provides legitimacy and authority to speak on a particular issue;
- a robust policy analysis, identifying solutions as well as problems;
- access to personal testimonies that illustrate the issues your campaign is highlighting.

## The importance of policy preparation

Within the Tenancy Deposits Campaign, Citizens Advice and Shelter had the following three strands in place:

- Significant programme experience, derived from the network of Bureaux, that showed clear evidence of a problem. In this case, the analysis was also backed by other authoritative sources (such as research conducted by the Office of National Statistics).
- Specific policy recommendations that were drawn from investigation into schemes operating in other countries. The solution advocated by Citizens Advice was for the establishment of a statutory custodial deposit scheme, in which money from deposits was to be held in a central pot from which either party could subsequently make a claim at the end of the tenancy, with any dispute between landlord and tenant to be resolved by arbitration. This proposal represented a self-financing solution that was demonstrably not only workable, but already working in similar contexts overseas.
- Personal testimonies, coordinated through the gathering of case study information by the staff of Citizens Advice Bureaux and Shelter. Those tenants affected were given support in presenting their own stories and highlighting their own concerns with local MPs and media.

This campaign successfully united these three different policy strands, presenting an obvious problem and a clear solution, backed by both macro-policy analysis and individual case studies. Key to this was the groundwork. Evidence from each of these strands was built up over many years prior to the launch, at the time when the Housing Bill was announced, of a more proactive and visible campaign that combined high level lobbying of Ministers and officials by Citizens Advice and Shelter staff, a postcard campaign run by bureaux and the 'email your MP' initiative run through the Shelter website, together with the active engagement of students (many of whom were affected by the issue) in partnership with the NUS.

Whilst this book isn't a guide to good research, your campaign will almost certainly be built on your own experience of an issue. It is likely that your policy analysis will be derived from this. It's worth noting here that your analysis is likely to depend on who participates in supplying and interpreting the information and learning the lessons from it.

Secondary sources from which relevant policy information can be derived, include for example:

---

**Potential secondary data sources for policy research**

- Has research been conducted by think tanks (for a list see for example Demos' Research Gateway at www.demos.co.uk), or by other VCOs with an interest in the issue?
- Are there relevant publications from seminars, workshops, etc. or in specialist media publications?
- Is there relevant information available from the Office of National Statistics (www.statistics.gov.uk)?
- What information is there as a result of Parliamentary scrutiny, such as Select Committee Reports www.publications.parliament.uk/pa/cm/cmselect.htm?
- What official reports are available, e.g. by the relevant Government department?

---

### 12.4.3 Marketing research

There may well be information that you need that is not available from the (secondary) sources identified above, especially in relation to public campaigning on your issue. In this case, new (primary) research may be needed.

This can be of two types:
- qualitative research – small numbers, probed in depth through a discussion style and open questions ['what do you think of ...?']
- quantitative research – large numbers, highly structured questionnaire, normally using closed [yes/no or multiple choice] questions

## Approaches in gathering information through marketing research

| Approach | How it works | Use |
|---|---|---|
| Qualitative research | This type of research includes focus groups and in-depth interviews. Information gathered tends to be impressionistic and subtle and is therefore reliant on the skills of the researcher. | • This method can be useful in exploring how prospective or actual issues and campaign messages are interpreted and assimilated by different audiences (which will often prove to be in ways other than expected).<br>• Qualitative research methods can also be deployed to gauge reactions to proposed campaign materials as well as actual examples of campaign coverage, in the media for example. |
| Quantitative research | This type of research includes surveys, opinion polls and questionnaires.<br><br>Findings can be subjected to analysis using statistical tools. | • These can be used in tracking public audiences' response through longitudinal research i.e. repeated surveys (see Section 11.2.1 on proxy measures), although bear in mind that you should get a response from your target audience, not the general public (unless the general public is your target audience, in which case see Section 13.1),<br>• A similar approach can be adopted with supporters/members.<br>• Some firms organise surveys of MPs too (e.g. nfpSynergy's Parliamentary Monitor).<br>• Polling can be used as a campaign tool but experience of its effectiveness is mixed (see Section 13.4). |

People tend to trust quantitative data more than they do qualitative information because it comes with greater certainty of statistical accuracy (as long as sampling is managed competently and the sample size is sufficiently big). However, for a number of reasons, findings from quantitative research may not be as representative of reality as they first appear:

- the way that questions are phrased, or even the way that response options are ordered will often affect the results (a disproportionate number of people tend to choose the first possible answer for example);
- there are also, notoriously, problems in understanding: how someone understands the question may not be the way that was anticipated;

**Properly conducted research, both qualitative and quantitative, can offer a great deal in the development, monitoring and evaluation of a campaign.**

- people are sensitive to current events so may react on the basis of something they read recently for example, so any snapshot obtained on a particular day may be influenced by unpredictable factors;
- there are also tendencies for people to give the answer they think the interviewer wants or that they see as being the 'right' answer to give – this has been used to explain why so many people famously said they were going to vote Labour in the 1992 general election before arriving at the polling booth only to put their x against the Conservative candidate.

Where budgets allow, however, properly conducted research, both qualitative and quantitative, can offer a great deal in the development, monitoring and evaluation of a campaign.

### 12.4.4 Internal reporting

You will also need to collect information that relates to your own organisation's campaigning capacity and constraints. The key areas that need to be considered when assessing your organisation's competence to campaign are examined in Section 8.2 on campaigning organisations, but this is mentioned here too, so that time and resources are allocated to carry out internal assessment. It needs to be a key component of an integrated campaign intelligence system.

---

### Comparative analysis

Whilst there is currently no obvious consensus about the factors that lead to effective campaigning, some of the process factors that make campaigning effective are captured in existing thinking, for example analysis that identifies the following success factors:
- clear and accessible programme logic (i.e. a thought-out version of how change is likely to happen);
- realistic and specific objectives;
- issue framed in terms of both short-term objectives and transformational goals;
- organisational legitimacy;
- work in coalitions and alliances;
- adapted strategies and tactics;
- joined up approach: campaigning as a set of parallel processes encompassing policy change, capacity building and opening up democratic spaces.

---

The table below outlines some of the points during a campaign where gathering specific campaign intelligence may be appropriate:

## Research and analysis in the campaign development process

| Stage in process | Campaigning environment | | Internal context | Policy |
|---|---|---|---|---|
| | Public | Targets and routes of influence | | |
| Analysing the issue and the context | Consider quantitative research to: <br> • define levels of public interest and support <br> • establish a baseline against which to measure progress <br> • help segment and target audiences | Consider the need for: <br> • research to identify the target, define the target's current stance and assess their susceptibility to change <br> • research to identify routes of influence and their stance on the issue, importance in the debate, and their own susceptibility to influence | Analyse internal capacities and constraints <br><br> Review as necessary | Ensure that initial research is robust and includes: <br> • evidence that provides legitimacy and authority to speak on a particular issue <br> • policy positions that can be persuasively advocated and defended <br> • personal testimonies to illustrate the case for change (wherever possible) |
| Developing strategy | Consider qualitative research to explore in greater depth audience perceptions and opinions in relation to the issue and the ways you propose to promote the campaign, and to identify possible routes into the debate | Consider undertaking additional research relating to specific routes of influence as identified | | |
| Setting objectives | Review evidence to ensure that objectives are realistic | | | |
| Implement-ation and monitoring | • consider qualitative research to test messages, materials, style, tone, etc. <br> • where feasible, commission longitudinal quantitative studies to track campaign progress | • monitor progress and continue to identify new opportunities through systematic environment scanning | | Any timetable of policy reports, etc. should ideally support and feed into the logic of the developing campaign, rather than dictating it |
| Evaluation | Pull together relevant information and fill any gaps | | | |

## 12.5 Managing the information

But in the end, it's not just about gathering the information; it's about making it accessible and useful. A good campaigning intelligence system should:

- capture useful details about the target institution and routes of influence;
- identify key players, ensuring records are updated, e.g. after cabinet reshuffles or after elections;
- record in note form when you meet/contact key influentials, and include information about their response;
- track the movement of key contacts between political bodies – you never know where a good contact or a foe may resurface later;
- record promises made by decision makers – this may come in useful several years after the promise has been made.

---

### Holding organisations to account

The Trade Justice Movement (TJM) is a coalition of international charities such as CAFOD, Oxfam and the World Development Movement, all campaigning for fairer world trade rules. At the time of writing, TJM is concerned that the European Union is about to embark on potentially damaging partnership agreements (called EPAs) with developing countries in Africa and the Caribbean. However, in 1998 the International Development Select Committee of the UK Parliament produced a series of recommendations to which the British Government should adhere in order to protect vulnerable producers in any future trade agreements with African or Caribbean countries. The TJM can use these previous recommendations to hold the current British Government to account and to insist that they live up to their previous promises when negotiating EPAs.

---

Obviously, the extent to which information management systems need to be in place for this to be administered effectively will depend on the size of the organisation. In bigger organisations a networked in-house database, managed by a gatekeeper who coordinates information and its use, may be needed to avoid duplication of effort and simultaneous approaches to the same target with conflicting messages. In the smallest organisation, a box file may suffice. Whatever the specific situation, any system needs to be backed by the necessary organisational buy-in to make it work.

Most books about campaigning go into some detail about political systems and how they work. This book puts forward the contention that it is more important to understand the need to gather the necessary information, to indicate sources and to encourage you to build your own campaign intelligence system in your own way. By developing a campaign intelligence system in this way, your organisation will be better equipped to campaign.

## Learning points

You may wish to consider the following:

✓ Effective campaigning organisations understand the context in which they operate, and how they can achieve impact by gathering intelligence systematically.
✓ Have you considered how a campaign intelligence system could benefit your campaign and your organisation?
✓ Is your system accessible and useful?

---

1. adapted from Kotler, P (1998) *Marketing Management: Analysis, Planning, Implementation & Control* (6th Edition). Prentice-Hall Intl Editions

# Part five:
# Change revisited

... in which we explain the premise that
campaigning must focus on achieving impact.

# 13 The dynamics of change

*"Up to now the philosophers have only interpreted the world in various ways; the point is, to change it."*
**Marx's 11th Thesis on Feuerbach**

There are many different theories of how change happens – some of these are explored below and their usefulness as tools in campaigning briefly assessed. As noted in section 11.2.5, whether or not they are explicit or thought out, all campaigns actually operate based on some kind of 'theory of change'.

In other words, every campaign is run, based on a set of assumptions as to:
 • how social and political change happens; and
 • how that particular campaign is going to have an influence on these processes.

One common set of assumptions in public campaigning, for example, looks something like the following:

**Standard model of change within which public campaigns tend to be fitted**

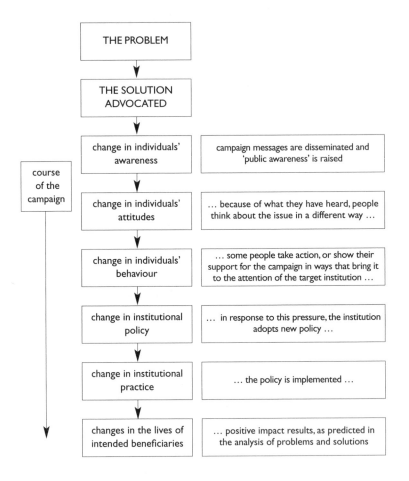

We believe that each of the links in this standard model is questionable.

## 13.1 Public awareness

The notion of public awareness is often bandied about within campaigning; but it is a problematic concept for two reasons – the terms 'public' and 'awareness'.

We have already noted (in Section 6.2) how the idea that, for any campaign, the target audience could be the public is unlikely to stand up to close scrutiny. Even general election campaigns, notionally targeted at every adult (except for convicted prisoners, the

Royal Family and members of the House of Lords), are increasingly narrowly targeted on the small percentage of swing voters who influence the election outcome in marginal constituencies.

'Awareness' is also a thorny term. It is rarely true that an individual can be said to lack awareness in relation to a particular issue. People experience issues in different ways. An individual may not know much about the issue, may not have a ready grasp of the facts, but in most cases it makes more sense to characterise this as representing a different awareness of the situation, one based on his or her own experience.

Generally speaking, the model of communications – top-down, information-based – derived from the assumption that you, the communicator, have awareness and that those you are attempting to reach through your communications don't work.

Instead, communication is most effective when it is a two-way process.

**Communication is most effective when it is a two-way process.**

## 13.2 Public attitudes

### 13.2.1 How attitudes change

People's attitudes are forged over many years and, as a consequence, tend to be more stable and difficult to alter than many campaigns assume. Over time, attitudes tend to coalesce in clusters and an entire belief system may have to be dismantled before someone will recognise a different reality to the one that they have built up from their experiences.

In effect, an individual's attitudes change only when he or she recognises that it is useful for him or her to do so. This tends to be as a reaction to feelings of dissonance, when inconsistency within or between attitudes is exposed.

Successful initiatives aimed at changing attitudes tend to involve techniques designed to induce this feeling of dissonance that then must be resolved. But because each attitude tends to be correlated with others, piecemeal change is difficult to achieve. It is rare for an overhaul of attitudes to take place. More commonly, new information is assimilated as an acceptable exception to the overall picture.

For example, while there is great public and political sympathy for children at risk of abuse, and a recognition that these children need protecting, these same children are swiftly demonised when their disturbed behaviour leads them into offending. At this point, they become perceived as criminals, worthy only of punishment not protection. People are unwilling, or unable, to make the obvious connections between the two sets of responses.

One other point is that – whilst it is generally recognised that a component of any attitude is cognitive (i.e. relating to a person's knowledge/beliefs) – it does not necessarily follow from this that you can influence someone's attitude by giving them new information. Someone who thinks that the government spends too much on the international aid budget, for example, may have a wildly over-exaggerated view of what that budget actually is. But telling them that the budget is in fact much lower than they assume won't necessarily help in any way to change, or even challenge, their underlying attitude that too much money is being spent on overseas aid.

They may disbelieve or distrust the figures you give them, or they may simply assimilate and rationalise them away. They may of course just choose to ignore you. This kind of attempt to expand their knowledge is unlikely to lead them to think that government money is being well spent and that that budget should not be cut.

Beliefs develop from, and are influenced by, attitudes as well as the other way round.

### 13.2.2 Why try to change attitudes?

Even if the difficult hurdles in changing attitudes are jumped, there is still a question to be answered: why do you want to change people's attitudes? If campaigning is about effecting meaningful change, a change of attitudes can never be an end in itself. It can be a short-term outcome, but only if it's clear how changing a person's attitudes will lead to their changing their behaviour. And that is anything but clear.

The idea that changing someone's attitude automatically leads to changing their behaviour is a simplistic one: the causal relationship is much more complicated than this. The theorists of behavioural psychology offer no clear guidance on this one. But the suggestion appears to be that, in many cases, rather than trying to change attitudes in the hope that this will lead to behaviour change, it might make more sense to present people with an incentive to change their behaviour or to legislate for them to do so. This approach is based on the anticipation that, after adopting the new behaviour, attitude change will follow.

> You may need to convince the target that you have enough public support for your position but you do not need to convince the whole world that you are right.

Even if you are convinced that changing attitudes is important, you need to remember that in campaigning you need to concentrate on changing the attitudes only of the people who can make a contribution towards the changes you advocate. This is never 'the public'. You may need to convince the target that you have enough public support for your position but you do not need to convince the whole world that you are right.

## 13.3 Behaviour

There are a range of theories that seek to explain the factors that influence a person's behaviour. Suggested variables affecting behaviour include the following:
- an intention to behave in a certain way
- the absence of environmental constraints preventing the behaviour
- the perception that the benefits of performing the behaviour outweigh the costs
- the extent to which performance of the behaviour is consistent with a person's self image
- a person's belief that he or she has the skills and abilities necessary
- social norms and social pressure

The implication of this is that campaigns should move away from seeking to change attitudes and move towards thinking about how to influence some of these other aspects underpinning behaviour. We are aware that social communications from the public sector often attempt to take this kind of approach and there is evidence, too, that campaigns in the US are beginning to adopt these kinds of techniques.[1]

### Communication as exchange[2]

Marketing theory posits an exchange between customers with needs and problems and marketers with solutions and resources. For the VCS, the challenge in campaigns is often to market an idea or a belief. This has been termed social marketing. In this model, the 'buyer' pays a price in terms of the time and effort involved in accepting the idea.

This is what capitalism has successfully mastered and campaigners need to understand the reasons for this success if they wish to invest effectively in campaigning for impact.

However, disadvantages that campaigners may face contrasted with those engaged in marketing for profit include that:
- they are often asked to influence non-existent or negative demand, and/or to promote 'benefits' that are invisible or only of benefit to third parties

> - there are invariably severely limited budgets and yet extravagant expectations (e.g. campaigns that run for a year where the aim is to change public opinion about some enormous and entrenched issue)
>
> What makes life even more difficult is that campaigners are often operating in an environment where there is a suspicion of marketing techniques. The effects of this may be to undervalue the usefulness of audience research and (possibly partly as a consequence of this) to over-emphasise moral messages that fail to resonate with key audiences.

## 13.4 Public influence on institutions

As well as thinking about the feasibility of mobilising public opinion and/or action it is obviously important to consider its desirability, i.e. to what extent will increased public support, even assuming you can develop it, have influence on the campaign target?

**You need to step outside the campaign and see what it looks like from your target audiences' point of view.**

After all, the extent of a positive correlation between mass opinion and institutional action can be hazy. The unprecedented size of the anti-war in Iraq march in February 2003 and the Government decision to act notwithstanding is just one, high profile, recent example.

This is of course a judgement call. But that judgement needs to be made based on clear thinking. You need to step outside the campaign and see what it looks like from your target audiences' point of view.

### Opinion polling: the Gambling Bill

The technique of using opinion polling to support your campaign is one that should be used with some caution. Although a way of generating media coverage, some opinion polls are unconvincing and the claim, based on polling, that, 'x per cent support y in the call for z' could be dismissed as meaning merely that 'x per cent of people don't necessarily have a strong opinion about z but if they are asked by y what they think about it, on a particular day, they will agree with y (whose position on the subject they suspect is z) that they support z too.'

One exception was the NOP poll commissioned by The Salvation Army in the early stages of its campaign on the Gambling Bill, which was still being quoted as definitive 12 months on. One important finding from the poll – that '3 per cent of the population thinks there are enough opportunities to gamble in Britain at the moment' – undercut the Government's key argument about the demand for expansion. But it would not have been effective had it not felt true as a representation of what people thought about the issue. It was a finding that – crucially – fitted with MPs' own experiences: no constituent was saying in surgery that they wanted more casinos, the only people calling for it were those with a vested economic interest.

There is also a danger that small amounts of visible support can be worse than none at all. If only a few people go on a demonstration or send filled-in fliers to a particular departmental target, it may be taken as sign that there is in fact little concern on the issue, and therefore that it doesn't need to move up the political agenda. And actions that bear the stamp of orchestration by a specific organisation or group (e.g. pre-written postcards) may be seen as something less than an authentic display of popular concern.

There's no formula. In a campaign context, public concern, like quality and beauty, is in the eye of the beholder, in other words it's anything that is **recognised by the target of a campaign** as being a legitimate manifestation of public concern on that particular issue.

As a rule of thumb there is likely to be a trade off between 'quality' and quantity of support – the easier the action, the more people are needed to take it for it to be seen as effective. It depends on the issue of course, and the target, but getting a hundred thousand signatures on a petition is unlikely to make the government think that you have that much real support behind your campaign, for example. Whereas five thousand letters to MPs from constituents almost certainly would.

**There is likely to be a trade off between 'quality' and quantity of support.**

## 13.5 The implementation gap: from policy to practice

**Campaigning victory should be equated with impact, not outcomes.**

A changed policy benefits people only if the policy is actually applied. And it should be noted that even the links between policy making and implementation can prove tenuous.

There can be a number of reasons why change in policy doesn't lead to actual change. The gap between stated policy and actual practice often remains great because of factors, such as:

- a lack of political will actually to implement the change
- an inability to implement the new policy, because of competing priorities or limited resources
- resistance to the new policy at the implementation level
- implementation of the policy in ways that were not expected when the policy was drawn up
- unexpected consequences impacting negatively on beneficiaries or others.

Maintaining political will can be vital during this stage. Campaigners often concentrate on getting policy changed but then do not follow through – they do not ensure that any changes are enforced and implemented. This is for understandable reasons: after all, it's difficult to maintain the pressure through implementation, especially if you want to claim campaign success at the policy change stage. Once that happens, people tend to assume that the issue is over, that victory has been achieved. But campaigning victory should be equated with impact, not outcomes. And policy change is a means to an end, not the end itself.

Neglecting the implementation stage of a campaign can be a sign that campaigners don't have their eye on the impact ball.

## 13.6 Alternative theories of change

The models presented below develop existing thinking on placing issue campaigning within a wider context of social and political change.

Some of these theoretical models described have been used in evaluating campaigns where no clear objectives were originally set, or where they were flawed for some reason. So it is possible to overlay a particular theory of how change happens over the campaign when assessing its progress. And these theories can be applied as a framework for developing campaigns as well as evaluating them.

Like all models, the ones outlined below represent a simplified version of reality. The idea that there is a straightforward linear progression in social and political change is simplistic. However, generic models such as the ones described below may have a use in that they can help in:

- identifying an overall approach
- making a broad assessment of the extent of progress towards a policy goal.

## 13.7 Stage model of policy change

In some circumstances, it may make sense to plot the stages an issue goes through within the policy process. This might look like the following:[3]

| Stage in change | What this means |
|---|---|
| Getting the issue on to, or higher up, the agenda | The first step is often to be noticed, even if, at this stage, people don't necessarily agree with what you're saying. |
| Influencing the debate | As your arguments build momentum, you may find it easier to get across your comments and opinions. You may even begin to hear others describing the issue on your terms. |
| Securing commitments to change | Decision makers and other campaign targets may make public statements of support, allowing you to hold them to account. |
| Formulation and enactment | A change in law or procedure takes place. |
| Implementation | A changed policy benefits people only if the policy is actually applied. There can be a number of reasons why change in policy doesn't actually lead to change in behaviour. Maintaining political will can be vital during this stage. |
| Change in people's lives | There may be all kinds of actual changes in people's lives resulting from the steps above, both intended and unintended. |

Of course this is a simplification, and the process isn't one-way.

## Advances are not linear or one-way

Like all models, this model outlining the stages in policy change should be used discerningly in thinking about campaign progress. Campaigns rarely progress from step to step along a forward path without setbacks along the way. To take just one example, the experience of the Empty Homes Agency's campaign on compulsory leasing suggests the following:

- just because officials initially reject your suggestions, it doesn't mean that the Department won't come round to your way of thinking
- just because a particular Minister comes out in support of your campaign aim, it doesn't mean that the Department is on board – reshuffles happen!
- just because you have built broad cross-party support for your campaign aim, it doesn't mean your issue will make it into the draft Bill
- and just because your issue is not in the draft Bill, it doesn't mean that it won't make its way into the Act during its passage through Parliament.

## 13.8 Mapping arenas of change

A broadly similar approach takes as its starting point an under-standing that campaign progress can be marked by the changing relationships between the range of organisations and groups with which you are working, or which you are trying to influence.

Ways of measuring how these relationships develop could (for example) assess the following factors; their:[4]

- level of familiarity with your network/organisation
- level of knowledge about your issue
- level of respect for your credibility
- level of willingness to engage (e.g. how willing to meet and to share information
- level of agreement with your position on the issue
- level of support demonstrated.

An early assessment of key audiences against these kinds of criteria can help in campaign development and provide baseline data against which to track progress.

For each audience, at periodic intervals, you could use a simple 1–5 scoring system against each criterion (backed by supporting evidence) to give an idea of the extent to which the campaign is progressing (or not).

### Arenas of change

| AUDIENCES Might include, for example: | familiarity | knowledge | respect | willingness to engage | agreement | support |
|---|---|---|---|---|---|---|
| Beneficiaries | | | | | | |
| Affected communities | | | | | | |
| Business | | | | | | |
| NGOs | | | | | | |
| Academics/ think tanks | | | | | | |
| Local authority | | | | | | |
| Central government | | | | | | |
| [others] | | | | | | |

## 13.9 Tracking target audience reaction

This approach, building on the product lifecycle model used extensively in marketing, involves tracking the progress of the campaign in terms of the reaction of a particular target audience to a campaign proposition.

Again, in this model, there can be said to be a number of stages through which a campaign tends to travel:[5]

1. Campaign proposition comes to target's attention.
2. Resources are mobilised around the arguments both for and against the campaign proposition.
3. In certain key arenas, there is debate around solutions.
4. Resolution occurs. This may mean (a) the solution being adopted, institutionalised and accepted, or (b) a realisation of the costs in making progress, a subsequent decline in concern, and the disappearance of the issue as one about which audiences are concerned, or (c) something in between whereby the issue gradually fades away.

Based on a range of quantitative data and anecdotal evidence (relating for example to media coverage, mentions in Parliament, change in public perceptions, the progress of the campaign can be plotted.

This can be helpful as a measure of progress and also as a monitoring and evaluation tool. In the latter case it would need to backed by a wider assessment of the extent to which any trends might reasonably be correlated with and thus possibly attributable to your own campaign efforts.

## The Gambling Bill

One interesting aspect of the campaign to influence the Gambling Bill was the way it suddenly changed from a policy issue into a political issue. When it became front page news in the *Daily Mail* and other newspapers, the debate was no longer about policy: it was about the political imperative of the Government finding resolution. One problematic aspect of this for The Salvation Army's campaign was that everything was up for grabs again, with the gambling industry attempting to roll back gains already made.

One key element of The Salvation Army's position during this highly politicised stage of the debate was to resist the entrancement of being close to power. The temptation can be to start playing the political game. But even if campaigners are as good at this as the politicians and corporate lobbyists (which may not be the case), the risk is that such an approach risks losing what gives the sector its legitimacy and unique value.

Given the pressure of extremely limited resources (in contrast to the lobbying from the gambling industry); although now an actor embroiled in a highly political issue, The Salvation Army resolved to continue to play to its strengths:

- that, crucially, The Salvation Army had no vested interest in the Bill, in stark contrast to its opponents;
- that the gambling industry in many respects represents an ideal target, often straightforwardly portrayed by the media as a shameless campaign 'villain'; and that there was no public support for the changes proposed.

## Campaign issue lifecycle

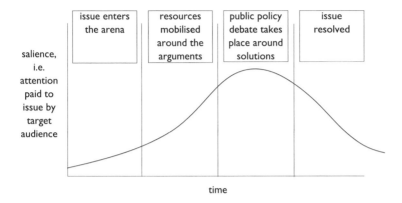

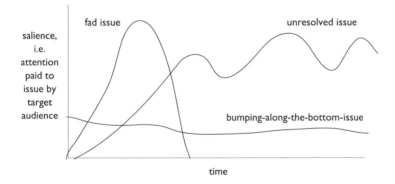

## 13.10 A rational overview of the policy process

The rational model describes a logical sequence of policy making in which change is said to occur as a result of something along the following lines:[6]

**Rational model of policy making**

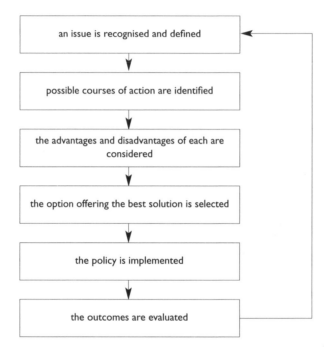

This model offers clear opportunities for campaigning influence at each stage.

If this were the way that policy was implemented, then campaigning would be a relatively straightforward discipline, like rocket science (where through a series of carefully managed incremental steps and the application of the basic laws of physics the project is brought to a conclusion and a rocket is successfully launched).

## 13.11 Change is chaotic

But of course it's not that simple. Perhaps not surprisingly, the rational model outlined above is generally rejected in terms of its relevance to how policy change actually happens. Alternative theories tend to emphasise policy making as a political process in which typically:[7]

- there is a general absence of innovation, with a relatively narrow focus on a few policy options, to deal with immediate problems
- routes of influence are manifold and various, from the direct (e.g. lobbying Ministers and officials) to the indirect and long-term (e.g. influencing the terms of the debate)
- policy change occurs as a function of the diverse actors and/or groups of actors found within the policy-making system, including, for example, officials, academics, VCOs, leading practitioners, researchers and other policy specialists
- a complex mix of interests and belief systems drive change.

Within this complexity, a policy innovation is more likely to happen when:

- a particularly influential group forces an issue higher up the agenda
- there is a consensus within an institution or wider network that change is needed.

This presents a view of social and political change as being driven by unpredictable forces that campaigners must try to control or ride.

On one level, Newton's laws of mechanics provide the basis for thinking about how to move campaigns forward and how social, as well as motive, change occurs:

1. Every body continues in rest, or uniform motion, until it is compelled to change that state by forces impressed upon it. (If you want change, you're going to have to exert pressure to achieve that change.)
2. Change in motion is proportional to the motive force impressed. (The more pressure you are able to mobilise, the more leverage you are likely to be able to exert.)
3. To every action there is always an equal and opposite reaction. (People will oppose you and not just stand idly by as you campaign for change.)

But just as Newton's laws are sufficient to explain everyday situations but do not represent the full picture (if, for example, you were travelling at the speed of light and/or were the size of a sub-atomic particle), so the idea of campaigning as something that is susceptible to linear explanation does not have universal applicability.

## Jumping through the policy window

One model[8] identifies three streams within policy agenda setting:
* **the Problem Stream** – this relates to information about 'real world' problems as well as feedback from past policies. (This stream is fairly volatile with change occurring as environmental conditions alter.)
* **the Political Stream** – this includes factors such as turnover of key administrators and legislators, and ideological contests within and between political parties. (Change results from shifts of power, internal power struggles, elections, etc.)
* **the Policy Stream** – comprising communities of researchers, campaigners and other specialists analysing problems and proposing solutions. (This stream is the least vulnerable to fluctuation.)

According to this model, the Government agenda is set in the Political and Problem Streams. Changes in these streams create 'policy windows', which allow for the rise and fall of issues on the public and policy agendas. Successful campaigns (operating in the Policy Stream) form linkages between the three streams and bring them together. They attach the policy to the problem to create the political conditions for policy makers to 'jump through the policy window' (in other words, to revise policy).

In this model, to be successful those seeking to influence policy must have:
* legitimacy
* political connections or negotiating skill
* persistence

## Model of policy agenda setting

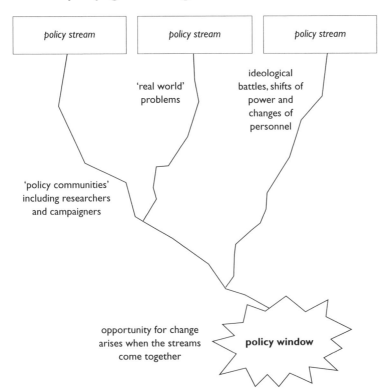

policy stream

policy stream

policy stream

ideological battles, shifts of power and changes of personnel

'real world' problems

'policy communities' including researchers and campaigners

opportunity for change arises when the streams come together

**policy window**

### Asylum vouchers campaign

As part of the 1999 Asylum and Immigration Bill, the UK Government introduced (in April 2000) a new national voucher scheme for asylum seekers. Asylum seekers were to qualify for 70–80 per cent of benefit levels and to receive the vast majority of their benefit not in cash but in vouchers redeemable only in certain stores. The voucher scheme also did not allow for change to be given following a purchase made with a voucher. A joint campaign by Oxfam, the TGWU and the Refugee Council ran until the scrapping of vouchers in April 2002. The Policy Agenda Setting model helps explain this quick turnaround.

In the problem stream, there was growing evidence that the vouchers scheme was an administratively flawed policy. It was expensive and difficult to administer and the fact that it did not work well was a fundamental cause of the subsequent change in policy. Of particular importance was that the hoped-for reduction in asylum seeker numbers as a result of this tough stance (designed to reduce the so-called pull factor) was not forthcoming.

In the political stream, the Minister involved had much invested in the scheme, and was personally associated with it. Change was politically feasible only after the appointment of a new Minister who was prepared to take a more pragmatic approach, and a 'cooling off' period so that accusations of a U-turn could be avoided. Movement of personnel at the Home Office was therefore almost certainly an essential prerequisite of policy change.

In conjunction with this, the campaign – in the policy stream – was effective in:

- exerting continued pressure through an astute focus on, and exploitation of, key influencing channels, e.g. through Labour Party structures
- producing timely and robust research that delivered clear evidence of hardship and discrimination (in the Token Gestures Report, issued in December 2000)
- building a broader network of support (involving organisations like the Local Government Association, the British Medical Association, children's organisations, etc.) that created just the kind of 'big tent' to which the Government was likely to react positively
- maintaining an excellent sense of timing in bringing the three streams together (crucially this included periods of 'holding off' and of policy engagement, for example, where the more obvious approach might have been to trumpet opposition from the sidelines)

adapted from *Review and Evaluation of Oxfam's Asylum Vouchers Campaign* by Jim Coe & Tess Kingham, May 2002. Thanks to Oxfam for permission to quote from this report.

## Learning point

Developing a deepening understanding of how change happens – and how your organisation can effectively intervene in the process of change – will ensure your campaigns have greater impact

## 13.12 Passion

All models simplify reality, that's why they're useful (although they should be discarded when the simplification becomes a distortion of reality). The impact-based campaign cycle that forms the basis of this book provides a sound basis for developing and delivering effective campaigns. But it is itself something that can be superceded.

Characteristics of a typical campaign include unpredictability, rapidity of change and sensitivity to small changes in initial conditions. The trick of the effective campaigner is to exploit these conditions, to harness limited resources to deliver exponential effects. This requires the ingenuity of the alchemist as much as the certainties of the physicist.

The best campaigners combine:

- a strong sense of strategy and planning – derived from a sophisticated assessment of the social and political environment in which they are operating and a realistic view of internal capacity and constraints
- a deep-rooted awareness of context – the ability to identify and exploit opportunity as it arises, based on an understanding of how change happens
- but above all passion – the belief in and commitment to what they are doing and the tenacity to keep on doing it

This can be summed up in the following model:

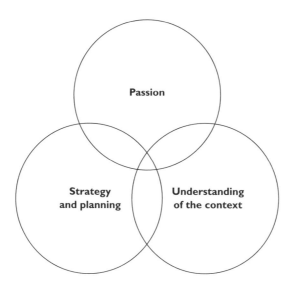

Passion on its own can sometimes be enough but, without the other two ingredients, campaigning success is usually down more to luck than judgement.

Campaigns can be made to work where two of the three qualities come together. But the heart of effective campaigning is the point at which all three converge. That is when campaigning has most impact.

This book cannot supply the passion that comes from within. But what we have tried to do is suggest ways of thinking about campaign planning, and ways of developing an understanding of the context within which change happens.

We hope it is useful and would welcome all feedback.

1. Coffman, J (2003) *Lessons in Evaluating Communications Campaigns: Five Case Studies.* Communications Consortium Media Center
2. Kotler, P and Andreasen, A (1996) *Strategic Marketing for Non-Profit Organizations* (5th Edition). Prentice Hall
2. adapted from Roche, C (1999) *Impact Assessment for Development Agencies: Learning to Value Change.* Oxfam. p198 and
   Keck, M and Sikkink, K (1998) *Activists Beyond Borders: Advocacy Networks in International Politics.* Cornell University Press. p25
3. adapted from Centre for Development and Population Activities (1999) *Advocacy: Building Skills for NGO Leaders.* CEDPA, Washington DC
4. adapted from Bryson, J M (1995) *Strategic Planning for Public and Nonprofit Organizations* (Revised Edition). Jossey-Bass. p252 and
   Coxall, B (2001) Pressure Groups in British Politics. Pearson Education Ltd. p157
5. Sutton, R (1999) *The Policy Process: An Overview*, Working Paper #118. Overseas Development Institute
6. from see 5. above
   Stone, D et al (2001) *Bridging Research and Policy: Background Paper presented to DFID-funded International Workshop.* Warwick
   Neilson, S (2001) *IDRC-Supported Research and its Influence on Public policy Knowledge, Utilization and Public Policy Processes: A Literature Review.* Evaluation Unit, IDRC
7. Kingdon's model as described in 6. above

# Glossary – some definitions

**action/activity** – a task or group of tasks undertaken

**AIDA** – formula of elements to include in campaigns; it stands for: attention, interest, desire, action

**aim** – a definition of the overall purpose of your campaign

**baseline assessment** – the collection of data before the campaign begins that can be used to compare with a study of the same characteristics carried out later

**beneficiaries** – those whose lives (it is intended) will be improved by the successful achievement of your campaign aim

**campaign cycle** – a framework for managing the different processes in the lifetime of an issue campaign

**campaigning** – the mobilising of forces by organisations to influence others in order to effect an identified and desired social, economic, environmental or political change

**campaigns** – organised actions around a specific issue seeking to bring about changes in the policy and behaviours of institutions and/or specific public groups

**demographics** – tangible characteristics about the target audience that can be recorded such as age, gender, occupation etc.

**double loop learning** – taking a 'double look' at the situation by questioning the relevance of accepted ways of operating norms

**drip drip approach** – a subtle, gradual approach to campaigning

**effectiveness** – focusing on and accomplishing the right things

**efficiency** – making the most economical use of resources

**evaluation** – an assessment of the performance of the campaign against expectations and its stated objectives

**impact** – the significant or lasting changes in people's lives that result from a particular course of action

**indicators** – markers chosen for measuring progress against campaign objectives

**inputs** – resources used in delivering the campaign

**influence map** – identifying everyone who may affect the policy process related to an issue

**means of verification** – sources and techniques used to gather evidence in monitoring and evaluation

**monitoring** – the ongoing process of gathering information on the progress of the campaign towards the achievement of its objectives

**objectives** – the desired results that will lead to the achievement of the campaign aim (each objective should be stated in a way that makes it possible to assess whether or not it has been achieved)

**outcomes** – the effects the campaign has actually had; the changes it has brought about, or helped bring about

**outputs** – what is generated by an activity or range of activities (e.g. a meeting with officials, or a physical object such as a campaign poster)

**PEST analysis** – a template used to assess external factors – political, economic, social and technological

**psychographics** – the collective essence of an individual's attitudes, beliefs, opinions, fears etc. that govern how he/she behaves

**power analysis chart** – dividing your influencers into known allies, opponents and undecided

**primary data** – data collected through your own research

**saturation approach** – blitzing your key targets with your campaign messages, hitting them from as many angles as possible within a short timescale

**secondary data** – information that is already available elsewhere

**segmentation** – a defined group of the organisation's target audience

**SMART objectives** – formula for setting objectives (specific, measurable, achievable, realistic and time-related)

**SWOT analysis** – an assessment technique looking at strengths, weaknesses, opportunities and threats

**target** – the individual or group who needs to change in order for the campaign aim to be achieved

**VCO** – voluntary and community organisation

**VCS** – voluntary and community sector

# Bibliography

Alinsky, SD (1989) *Rules for Radicals: A Pragmatic Primer for Realistic Radicals*, Vintage Books: Random House

Amnesty International (2001) *Campaigning Manual*, Amnesty International Publications at www.amnesty.org/campaign/campaignresources.html

Bowers, L (2002) *Campaigning With Attitude*, at www.payback.org.uk

Brown, DL and Fox, J (2000) *Transnational Civil Society Coalitions and the World Bank: Lessons From Project and Policy Influence Campaigns*, IDR Reports Vol 16 No 1

Bryson, JM (1995) *Strategic Planning for Public and Nonprofit Organizations* (Revised Edition), Jossey-Bass

Campaign to Protect Rural England (2002) *Getting Organised & Getting Results, CPRE* at www.cpre.org.uk/publications/CPRE/campaigning.htm

Centre for Development & Population Activities (1999) *Advocacy: Building Skills for NGO Leaders*, CEDPA, Washington DC

Chapman, J and Wameyo, A (2001) *Monitoring and Evaluating Advocacy: A Scoping Study*, ActionAid

Chapman, J and Fisher,T (1999) *The Thoughtful Activist: A Toolkit for enhancing NGO Campaigning and Advocacy* New, Economics Foundation

Chisnall, P (1975) *Marketing: A Behavioural Analysis*, McGraw-Hill

Chisnall, P (1992) *Marketing Research* (4th Edition), McGraw-Hill

Church, M *et al* (2003) *Participation, Relationships and Dynamic Change: New Thinking on Evaluating the Work of International Networks*, Development Planning Unit, University College London

Coe, J and Smith, H (2003) *Action Against Small Arms: A Resource & Training Handbook*, International Alert, Oxfam GB & Saferworld

Coffman, J (2003) *Lessons in Evaluating Communications Campaigns: Five Case Studies*, Communications Consortium Media Center

Cohen, D, de la Vega, R and Watson, G (2001) *Advocacy for Social Justice: A Global Action and Reflection Guide*, Kumarian Press Inc

Covey, J (1994) *Accountability and Effectiveness of NGO Policy Alliances*, IDR Reports Vol 11, No 8

Coxall, B (2001) *Pressure Groups in British Politics*, Pearson Education Ltd

Davies, R (2001) *Evaluating the Effectiveness of DFID's Influence with Multilaterals: Part A, A Review of NGO Approaches to Evaluation of Advocacy Work*, DFID

Fowler, A (1997) *Striking a Balance: A Guide to Enhancing the Effectiveness of Non Governmental Organisations in International Development*, Earthscan

Goffman, E (1974) *Frame Analysis: An Essay on the Organization of Experience*, Harper & Row

Grant, W (2000) *Pressure Groups & British Politics*, Macmillan Press Ltd

Handy, C (1993) *Understanding Organizations* (4th Edition), Penguin Books

Hubert, D (2000) *The Landmine Ban: A Case Study in Humanitarian Advocacy*, The Thomas J Watson Jr Institute for International Studies

Hudson, M (2002) *Managing Without Profit: The Art of Managing Third-sector Organizations* (2nd Edition), Directory of Social Change

Iliffe, S (2004) *The Good Membership Guide for the Voluntary Sector*, NCVO

International Fund for Agriculture Development (2002) *Managing for Impact in Rural Development: A Guide for Project M&E*, IFAD

Johnson, G and Scholes, K (1989) *Exploring Corporate Strategy: Text & Cases*, Prentice Hall International (UK) Ltd

Jordan, G and Maloney, W (1997) *The Protest Business? Mobilizing Campaign Groups*, Manchester University Press

Kakabadse, A, Ludlow, R and Vinnicombe, S (1988), *Working in Organizations*, Penguin Books

Keck, M and Sikkink, K (1998) *Activists Beyond Borders: Advocacy Networks in International Politics*, Cornell University Press

Kelly, L (2002) *Research and Advocacy for Policy Change: Measuring Progress*, Foundation for Development Cooperation

Kotler, P (1988) *Marketing Management: Analysis, Planning, Implementation & Control* (6th Edition), Prentice-Hall Intl Editions

Kotler, P and Andreasen, A (1996) *Strategic Marketing for Non-Profit Organizations* (5th Edition), Prentice Hall

Lamb, B (1997) *The Good Campaigns Guide*, NCVO Publications

Lattimer, M (2000) *The Campaigning Handbook* (2nd Edition), Directory of Social Change

Lyford J, Jones, R and Goggin, K (2002) *Promoting Self-Evaluation: Action Research Project Report*, Community Fund NE Region

Miller, V and Covey, J (1997) *Advocacy Sourcebook: Frameworks for Planning, Action and Reflection*, Institute for Development Research

Morgan, G (1998) *Images of Organization (The Executive Edition)*, Berrett-Koehler Publishers Inc & Sage Publications Inc.

Neilson, S (2001) *IDRC-Supported Research and its Influence on Public Policy Knowledge Utilization and Public Policy Processes: A Literature Review*, Evaluation Unit, IDRC

Peters, T and Waterman, R (1982) *In Search of Excellence*, Harper & Row

Peters, T (1988) *Thriving on Chaos: Handbook for a Management Revolution*, Macmillan London

Plantz, M, Greenway, M T and Hendricks, M (1997) *Outcome Measurement: Showing Results in the Nonprofit Sector*, at http://national.unitedway.org/outcomes/library/ndpaper.cfm

Policy Project (1999) *Networking for Policy Change: An Advocacy Training Manual*, Policy Project, Washington DC

Pugh, D and Hickson, D (1996) *Writers on Organization* (5th Edition), Penguin Books

Roche, C (1999) *Impact Assessment for Development Agencies: Learning to Value Change*, Oxfam

Rockefeller Foundation Communication and Social Change Network (2001) *Measuring and Evaluating Communication for Social Change*, Communication Initiative Forum

Save The Children (1999) *Working for Change in Education: A Handbook for Planning Advocacy*, SCF

Sharma, R R (1999) *An Introduction to Advocacy: Training Guide*, SARA/AED

Sprechmann, S and Pelton, E (2001) *Advocacy Tools and Guidelines: Promoting Policy Change*, CARE

Stone, D *et al* (2001) *Bridging Research and Policy: Background paper presented to DFID-funded International Workshop*, Warwick University.

Sun T (1981) *The Art of War*, Hodder & Stoughton

Sutton, R (1999) *The Policy Process: An Overview, Working Paper #118*, Overseas Development Institute

United Nations Development Programme Evaluation Office (2002) *Handbook on Monitoring and Evaluating For Results*, UNDP

van Tuijl, P and Jordan, L (1999) *Political Responsibility in Transnational NGO Advocacy*, Bank Information Center, Washington DC

VeneKlasen, L with Miller, V (2002) *A New Weave of Power, People & Politics: The Action Guide for Advocacy & Citizen Participation*, World Neighbors

Wilson, D (1984) *Pressure: The A to Z of Campaigning in Britain*, Heinemann Educational Books

Wilson, R, Gilligan, C and Pearson, D (1996) *Strategic Marketing Management*, Butterworth-Heinemann Ltd

WK Kellogg Foundation (1998) *Evaluation Handbook: Philosophy & Expectations*, WK Kellogg Foundation

WK Kellogg Foundation (2001) *Logic Model Development Guide*, WK Kellogg Foundation

Wolf, K (2001) *Now Hear This: The Nine Laws of Successful Advocacy Communications*, Fenton Communications

# Appendix – campaigning and political activities by charities

Brian Lamb, Director of Communications at RNID writes:

This section looks at the practical steps that you might need to take to ensure that your organisation complies with the Charity Guidelines CC9 Campaigning and Political Activities by Charities (version 09/04) issued by the Charity Commission. The guidance can be accessed from their website at www.charity-commission.gov.uk.

## Background

The guidelines were substantially revised following the Government's Strategy Unit report *Private Action, Public Benefit* which highlighted the benefits of charities' advocacy and campaigning role. The report supported charities' political role noting that they played a crucial role in the political process because their strong links to the community meant they where well placed to comment on the effects of Government policy. It also affirmed that the high levels of trust and confidence enjoyed by charities ensured that they are well placed to offer alternative ways of engaging with public policy and enhancing democracy and that the diversity of causes they represented enables charities to give voice to a wider range of political perspectives.

## The context for campaigning

The guidelines make clear that charities cannot be constituted to pursue political purposes. However campaigning and political activity can be carried out as a means of furthering their charitable purposes.

Campaigning and political activity are seen as distinct by the Commission with the latter confined to activities which advocate or oppose changes in the law or public policy. In either case these activities are governed by the same rules.

The crucial issues that trustees and staff within an organisation have to consider in pursing campaigning or political activities are:

- that the activities are relevant to the purposes of the charity as set out in the governing documents

- that they are an effective means of furthering the purposes of the charity
- that the resources applied are proportional with achieving the aims of the campaign

The trustees also have to assess the reputational risk associated with any of the activities and comply with any other laws and regulations that relate to these areas of activity.

The most relevant separate guidance in this area is the British Code of Advertising, Sales Promotion and Direct Marketing (The CAP Code) which is administered by the Advertising Standards Authority. See www.asa.org for a full list of the statutes and regulations affecting advertising and promotions in England and Wales.

Charities can devote whatever proportion of their resources to campaigning that they think is appropriate to achieve their stated purposes. However, where the campaign is political, defined by aiming to seek a change to the law or public policy, trustees must ensure that these do not become the dominant means by which they carry out their purposes. Where political activities become the dominant means by which a charity carries out its activities there will become a question of whether a charity is acting outside of the trusts.

The Commission's guidance puts a great deal of emphasis on the management of risk associated with campaigning though there is no particular reason to see campaigning as involving greater risks than for other areas of managing a charity's reputation.

## How to organise campaigning to meet the requirements

You need to think carefully about how you set the objectives for campaigns, how you implement them, who you work with and what control you have over alliances and partners and how you will demonstrate that the outcomes are relevant to your objects and purposes. By following many of the process outlines in early chapters of this guide you will be well placed to do this, but there are some specific areas that you should keep in mind.

| Area | Issue | Action |
|---|---|---|
| **Charitable purposes** | | |
| The scope and benefits of engaging in a particular campaign | You should ensure that the campaign plans are clearly within the purposes of your charity as outlined in your governing document. This may be your Constitution, Memorandum and Articles of Association, Trust Deed or other legal instrument. You must be able to clearly demonstrate and link between the activity and the impact on the people or issue you are set up to address. | Review plans against purposes to ensure there is a fit and that you can demonstrate the positive impact of the proposed campaign on your cause. |
| **Use of campaign materials** | | |
| Evidence | The Commission recognises that many campaign communications such as newspaper advertising will not be able to give the full rationale for a campaign or the evidence to support this. However it does expect that such evidence could be produced and the charity trustees should be prepared to properly explain and defend their charity's decision to use campaigning to achieve its purposes. | Ensure that a clear plan is produced (see Section 5) and that this is approved by trustees. Good campaigning should in any case be based on sound evidence. |
| Emotive materials | The Guidelines recognise that charities work inevitably deals in emotive issues. However charities have to consider the particular risks that potently engaging in controversial issues can have for the reputation of the charity if there is a risk of adversely affecting the public's perception and attitude towards the charity. | Ensure that a risk analysis of the potential benefits and damage that could be caused by the use of emotive materials and that you have the evidence to back up any claims made in your materials. |
| **Campaign methods** | | |
| Demonstrations and direct action | Charities can use demonstrations and events to get across their views. This can include participation in marches, rallies, or peaceful picketing within the law. As with emotive materials charities need to consider the possible reputation risks that might arise from the type of action they are associating the charity with. Specifically you will need to consider how you will ensure that no public order offences are committed in the name of the charity. | Ensure that you have fully addressed how you will manage the risks associated with public order offences in the way the event is organised and participants are informed about what activities are acceptable and that the event is peaceful. If working with other organisations ensure that the event is fully under the control of the organiser. |

| Partnerships and coalitions | It is not realistic that everything an alliance does will fit with the charitable purposes of your own charity. However you are responsible for ensuring that the arrangement will further you purposes and how you manage any risks associated with the alliance having broader aims than your own. | Ensure that your plan includes a risk assessment of being involved in any coalitions and a clear strategy for how you will handle any conflicts between the alliance and your organisation. |
| --- | --- | --- |
| Research | Research needs to be relevant and robust using accepted and reputable research methods. Research that is not credible will run the risk of damaging the campaign and the charity's reputation. Charities are permitted to advocate the same policy solutions as political parties as long as it is in the furtherance of their own purposes. However charities are not permitted to support a political party or candidates. | Where possible ensure that only reputable research companies are commissioned. If using in-house resources ensure that valid research methods are followed. Do not make statements that cannot be fully substantiated from your evidence. |
| Contact with political parties | It is important to be able to demonstrate that the campaign activities are furthering the charity's purposes and that the money devoted to the activities has furthered the achievement of the charity's campaigns. | Check policies and statements to ensure that they only support the charity's purposes. You may wish to ensure that policy sign off takes place at a senior level within the organisation. Take particular care to ensure that when using the views of politicians these do not promote or imply support of the charity for that party. Ensure that the use of politicians fits within the overall strategy of the campaign so that there is no danger of inadvertently supporting a partisan message. |
| **Evaluation** | | |
| Measuring impact | | Ensure that there is a process in place to evaluate the campaign (see Section 5.2). Think about how this could be effectively communicated to supporters. More charities are using impact reporting as a means of showing how they are meeting their aims. |

If you follow the advice on planning and evaluating campaigning outlined in the preceding chapters you should meet most of the requirements for risk management in relation to campaigning. Of key importance is the relationship with your trustee body as they are responsible for the overall management of risk for the organisation. To discharge these obligations many charities now have development risk management strategies and they report on these as part of the fulfilment of the SORP reporting requirements. You should ensure that your charitable campaigns are routinely part of that risk management process.

# Feedback

We would very much appreciate your comments to help make future editions of this Good Campaigns Guide as relevant as possible.

1. How did you hear about this guide?

❏   My organisation
❏   Voluntary Sector magazine
❏   NCVO members' mailing
❏   Press coverage
❏   At an NCVO seminar/conference
❏   Advertisement
❏   Mailshot
❏   Recommendation
❏   Other, please state

2. How many people in your organisation will use this guide?

3. Which parts of the guide have you found most useful?

4. Why?

5. Which parts of the guide have you found least useful?

6. Why?

_____

_____

_____

_____


7. What additional information would be useful to include in future editions?

_____

_____

_____

_____


8. How would you rate the guide overall?

❏ Very useful
❏ Fairly useful
❏ Not very useful
❏ Not at all useful

9. We would appreciate your comments on the content, language and layout of the guide.

_____

_____

_____

_____


10. How will you use this guide?

❏ Inform myself
❏ Brief trustees
❏ Other, please specify

11. Which organisation do you represent (you do not have to give this information)

_____

12. Are you a

☐ Trustee
☐ Staff member
☐ Professional advisor
☐ Other, please specify

13. Is your organisation a member of NCVO?

☐ Yes
☐ No

14. What size organisation do you represent?

☐ Small charity (less than £100,000 income)
☐ Medium-sized charity (£100,000 - £1m income)
☐ Large charity (over £1m income)

15. Would you like to be sent information about membership and other services available from NCVO?

If so please give details

Name ........................................................................

Position ........................................................................

Organisation ........................................................................

........................................................................

Address ........................................................................

........................................................................

........................................................................

Tel/fax ........................................................................

Email ........................................................................

**Data protection**
The information you provide will be held in accordance with the Data Protection Act 1998 and will be used by NCVO and its agents to supply the services which you have requested. We may wish to contact you from time to time with information on other products and services available from us, which we believe will be of interest to you.
☐ If you would like to be contacted please tick here.